# More Praise for *That or Which, and Why*

"A brilliant and entertaining romp through difficult questions of English usage. As authoritative as it is witty, it belongs on the desk of every editor, writer, and student of the language."

**—Gene Roberts, former managing editor,**
*The New York Times*

"In *That or Which, and Why*, Evan Jenkins dishes out tough love for copy editing, giving myriad examples of the folly of following some grammar rules 'out the window.' Instead, he implores copy editors to fight the important fights, and gives air-tight reasoning and helpful memory tools to help in those battles. His advice is sound, and important."

**—Amy Carlile, Deputy Managing Editor,**
*Roll Call*

"Steering between word mavens who'll smack you for violating rules that went out with silent movies — if they were ever valid — and 'do your own thing' linguists and dictionary-makers, Evan Jenkins's *That or Which, and Why* offers sensible guidance with a firm but gentle hand."

**—Louis Trager, reporter and editor,**
**San Francisco Bay area**

"Evan Jenkins's new book is witty, wise, and passionate, but it is also refreshingly sensible. He goes further or farther (thankfully I now know it doesn't matter) to put usage into a context that makes sense. He also draws lines where they need drawing (who and whom still matter). Even when he treads where I am unwilling to go (either 'compared with' or 'compared to' is okay?), I have a grumbling suspicion he may be right. *That or Which, and Why* is a wonderful new companion to keep on my writing desk."

**—Tom Rosenstiel, Director,**
**Project for Excellence in Journalism**

"Even professed language experts are bound to learn something from *That or Which, and Why*. With wit, affection, and a good ear, Evan Jenkins tackles dozens of questions about precise English and sorts out which rules to follow, which to ignore, and why it all matters.

—**Kirk Arnott, Assistant Managing Editor,**
***The Columbus Dispatch***

"In *That or Which, and Why*, Evan Jenkins steers a beautifully pragmatic and wittily wise middle course between the fossilized 'purists' and the freewheeling 'anything goes' crowd regarding our native tongue. If you do not already have his *Language Corner* as one of your Web shortcuts, this volume is evidence you should — it's so blessedly reassuring to understand the 'why' of the 'what' when you want to persuade yourself and others that English is still very much alive and kicking."

—**Nancy Holeman Holmes, Division of General Studies,**
**Morris College**

"Evan Jenkins has no time for descriptivists or their profligate tolerance (see 'From whence'). He is just as short with prescriptivists' dull sanctimony (relish the testiness of "first annual"). With its assured voice and vivid images ('to be sure' is described as 'pince-nez professorial'), *That or Which, and Why* is a unique addition to worthy usage commentary."

—**Kannan Somasundaram, Chief Copy Editor,**
***Daily News & Analysis (DNA)*, Mumbai, India**

"Evan Jenkins's absorbing considerations about grammar, written in response to real questions and gripes from working journalists, educators and those who just love language, judiciously balance today's common sense with yesterday's rules. His advice can help any writer to be both clear and kind to readers."

—**Seth Wigderson, Professor of History,**
**University of Maine at Augusta**

# That or Which, and Why

# That or Which, and Why

A Usage Guide for Thoughtful Writers and Editors

## Evan Jenkins

Routledge
Taylor & Francis Group
New York   London

Routledge
Taylor & Francis Group
270 Madison Avenue
New York, NY 10016

Routledge
Taylor & Francis Group
2 Park Square
Milton Park, Abingdon
Oxon OX14 4RN

Routledge is an imprint of Taylor & Francis Group, an Informa business

Printed in the United States of America on acid-free paper
10 9 8 7 6 5 4 3 2 1

International Standard Book Number-10: 0-415-97726-6 (Softcover) 0-415-97725-8 (Hardcover)
International Standard Book Number-13: 978-0-415-97726-5 (Softcover) 978-0-415-97725-8 (Hardcover)

---

### Library of Congress Cataloging-in-Publication Data

---

Jenkins, Evan.
    That or which, and why : a usage guide for thoughtful writers and editors / Evan Jenkins.
      p. cm.
    Based on the author's "Language corner" column in the Columbia journalism review.
    ISBN 0-415-97725-8 (acid-free paper) -- ISBN 0-415-97726-6 (pbk. : acid-free paper)
    1. English language--Usage--Handbooks, manuals, etc. 2. English language--Errors of usage--Handbooks, manuals, etc. 3. English language--Grammar--Handbooks, manuals, etc. I. Columbia journalism review. II. Title.

PE1460.J46 2007
428.2--dc22
                                          2006025463

---

**Visit the Taylor & Francis Web site at**
**http://www.taylorandfrancis.com**

**and the Routledge Web site at**
**http://www.routledge.com**

# *Preface*

I would argue — I do, right here in this book, on page 100 — that it doesn't matter at all whether we use "more than" or "over" to describe something that is larger than something else. The distinction is arbitrary, a 19th-century invention that flies in the face of age-old custom among English speakers and adds needlessly to the burdens of writing and editing. There's more than one way to skin a cat, and for that particular cat "more than" and "over" make two perfectly fine ways.

On the other hand I would also argue, and do, that it matters a good deal whether we use "comprise" (page 33) to mean to encompass or embrace (yes) or to make up or compose (emphatically no). We should insist on that distinction, even amid increasing misuse as "comprise" enjoys faddish popularity. "Four buildings comprise the complex" is not literate.

Between those two poles lies a distinction we've been asked to make for some time now between "fewer" and "less" (page 51). Again, arbitrary, but trickier and harder to ignore than the "more than" versus "over" business, and less clear-cut than the matter of "comprise."

The rules that govern our use of English should make sense and be of practical utility. Often they can in fact be explained logically. Sometimes their only sense lies in their being so thoroughly established — so thoroughly idiomatic — that we can't defy them (but the definition of idiom changes, and is frequently open to argument).

And sometimes rules, even commonly accepted ones, make little sense when examined closely. Some of the topics discussed in this book fall into that category.

That distinction between "more than" and "over" is meaningless. The "rule" that we can't use a possessive noun (Toni Morrison's, for example) and follow it with a pronoun (her) began with a logical instinct and followed it all the way to absurdity (page 120). Such a restriction would require the rewriting not only of Morrison herself but of Shakespeare and Dickens, along with almost everyone else who has ever been published in English.

When logic points us toward literal-minded nonsense, the higher logic of sense has to take control.

Yet the distinction between "more than" and "over" is widely prescribed, as is the complication involving "that" and "which" (page 145). Even the silliness about possessives with pronouns seems to have found its way into at least one book at some point. So it's worthwhile to be familiar with such things; there are believers out there. In a better world such rules would (will?) be stricken from the list of things we need to pay attention to. Some hair-splitting and nit-picking are inevitable in writing and editing, but they shouldn't be our principal focus.

This is not a dictionary; it's far too selective for that. It's also more discursive and more openly judgmental (without arrogance, I trust) than most dictionaries can afford to be. Yet it is not just a compendium of do's and don'ts. As it has evolved — in an approach that I've used at various times in a long career — it has seemed to me to be a series of conversations.

The result is mostly a book about usage — preferred ways to use words (including "usage," page 154) and phrases, good choices about practices. With the long-winded exception of an essay on hyphens, it is not about punctuation, a can of worms I'd rather leave to others. (For concise, orderly examination of the problem I can enthusiastically recommend "The Well-Tempered Sentence," by Karen Elizabeth Gordon.)

Nor is the book about style in its most mundane sense; advice on whether to spell out or abbreviate "street" in addresses won't be found in these pages. Such choices are up to you, or to the people who put out your stylebook if you have one.

What I hope the reader will find here are persuasive answers to questions that arise in his or her work from day to day. Some answers will point out options the reader can weigh case by case: "farther" or "further"? (page 49); present tense or past? (Sequence of Tenses, page 133). I hope the guidance offered here will make those choices surer.

* * *

I began putting this collection together as Language Corner in the pages of the *Columbia Journalism Review* (*CJR*), where my title was senior editor. (I'm now a consulting editor there, and continue to write Language Corner.) One topic is covered in each issue of the magazine, which is published every other month and is the dean, so to speak, of American journalism criticism.

Those entries went on the Web (at http://www.cjr.org, Language Corner), and I added material there that had not appeared in the print version of *CJR*. For this book I've written a good many entries and made many revisions that have not appeared anywhere else. So while the book reflects ideas honed largely over a long career in 20th-century journalism, a fair amount of 21st-century thought informs it as well.

When I began Language Corner I naturally imagined an audience of journalists. From habit shaped as a supervising editor and newsroom teacher, the bulk of it in newspaper journalism, I pictured younger people, probably early- or mid-career editors but certainly thoughtful writers, too.

With such an audience in mind (it turned out to be much broader, and often older, than I had expected) I did not want to shout commands, and I did want to have some fun. This is not life and death. Above all I wanted to offer useful, practical information without the dogmatic, ipse-dixit rigidity of so many usage commentators. We should savor the language and find joy in it, not beat it into submission.

Because tension and timidity can cause people to follow "rules" straight out the window, I've tried to offer guidelines, not orders, where possible, and I've tried to say *why* something is as it is — or rather why I, based on learning and experience, see it as I do. No matter how doctrinaire the lecturer, an awful lot of the language laws we live by are subjective, way down deep.

The material for Language Corner and ultimately for this book came at first almost entirely from print journalism, with a bit here and there from radio and television. Quickly, though, I began to receive questions and suggestions from readers of *CJR* or the larger Web collection, and to illustrate the topics I frequently turned to databases. Perhaps a third of the entries contain the fruits of such searches.

The visitors e-mailed from all over the world — from Australia, Japan, South Korea, the Philippines, Malaysia, India, Bangladesh, the United Arab Emirates, Egypt, Russia, Germany, the Czech Republic, and England, among other foreign lands, and of course the United States and Canada (which is only half foreign). A majority of the correspondents were active in some way in journalism, but a sizable minority were not. They included lawyers, engineers, advertising and public-relations people, teachers, students, artists, medical professionals, quite a few civil servants, one labor-union activist in a developing nation, and at least one novelist.

The Internet age has its glories; those communications — except for an occasional "You idiot!" or a polite variation thereof — have been extremely gratifying and helpful. The "idiot!" notes, fortunately, have come only from people who were mistaken.

\* \* \*

Rules we must have. A thoughtful editor put that truth eloquently after coming down hard, in one installment of a continuing e-mail conversation, on a certain figure of speech. Referring to his argument in opposition to the phrase, he wrote:

> The only way to gainsay this is to declare the expression idiomatic and point to how widespread the use is. But the logical extension of this method seems to be descriptivism that can justify any popular barbarism.

Descriptivism can be dangerous. Boiled down to a gross exaggeration (never mind logical extensions) for purposes of illustration only, descriptivism scorns such influences as word derivation specifically and precedent generally, and instead jots down whatever more or less educated people are doing with the language this week and declares it correct, at least until next week. Dangerous indeed; the world really doesn't need "the battle wages" (page 123). At least not this week or next.

The opposite of descriptivism, and the other great camp among language scholars, is prescriptivism. It, too, can be dangerous. It accepts (gross illustration again) only those commandments graven in stone sometime before 1930. But the language does change and grow. It did so with very little outside discipline for nearly a millennium. Then, starting in the 18th century, the law-givers moved in. Their work was badly needed and has mostly been useful. But it has also produced rules that help not at all, that seem to exist only for their own sake — prescriptivism at its worst.

The advice in this volume is prescriptive at times and descriptive at others. Not surprisingly, it has been criticized occasionally by loyalists in both camps. I feel comfortable adopting, from the *New York*

*Times Manual of Style and Usage,* that most holy of axioms for writers and editors: The most important rule is the rule of common sense.

Despite differences in judgment that inevitably arise, I'm an enthusiastic fan of the we're-all-in-this-together approach to correction and education. Some years ago, conducting a seminar at one of the smaller New York Times Company newspapers, I found myself saying "we" might want to try this and "we" ought to avoid that. I hadn't planned it, but it seemed natural and sensible. The second-person plural appears frequently in this volume. We, writers and editors all, have to think through our problems.

* * *

This book should be easy to use, whether read straight through for the sheer ecstasy of it or consulted by topic as needed. The contents are arranged alphabetically with abundant cross-referencing, rather than in thematic sections. (Using thematic language books, I've found myself almost invariably looking first at the index, which is of course alphabetical.)

With examples from published journalism, I've chosen not to identify the outlets because I see no point in doing so. Nor do I identify those among my correspondents whose arguments I don't agree with, though I'm grateful to them for raising valuable questions. I use honorifics with names because they enhance civility, which seems a valuable end in itself.

I hope the book will be instructive — useful — and a kindly read. I apologize if the voice sounds exasperated at times. I once headed the principal copy desk of a sizable newspaper, *Newsday,* and later performed similar enforcement duty on deadline at a larger one, the *New York Times.* Irascibility was an occupational hazard in such work, and the reader may conclude that age has not entirely cured mine. But we're still in this together.

**E.J.**
*Jan. 10, 2007*

# A/An with Abbreviations;
# A Historic, etc.

## Sound Beginnings

Brendan Coyne, director of public information for Mount Saint Mary College in Newburgh, N.Y., wanted to double-check his understanding that "an" should be used in front of abbreviations that start with consonants but *sound* as if they start with vowels — for example, MSMC.

Mr. Coyne's understanding is correct. If the abbreviation is pronounced as a series of individual letters, the first letter determines the choice of article — "*a* U.S. overture" (a yew) but "*an* NSC study" (an en) and "*an* MSMC student" (an em).

With acronyms, multiword abbreviations that are pronounced as single words, the initial sound of the invented word dictates the choice of article. A force marshaled by the North Atlantic Treaty Organization is "*a* NATO force" (a nate). And from the United Nations Conference on Trade and Development we could have "*an* Unctad report" (an unk, no less).

There's confusion (or something) about the choice between "a" and "an" before "history," too. We don't run around talking about "isstory," so why should we drop the "h," in effect, and write "an history"? We shouldn't.

There's room for argument with "herb." But in American English the unaspirated "h" has prevailed for now, leading to "an herb."

And it is always, of course, an honor to serve.

# Adverb Placement

## *Try to Be Early*

Two schools of thought seem to exist on the placement of adverbs and adverbial phrases with compound verbs. One is easy: just stick it in front of all parts of the verb and be done with it. "He always has been a little slow," say, or "She frequently will disagree" or "That train habitually has run late."

The other approach, subscribed to here, is that the adverb (or adverbial phrase) tends to work more mellifluously after the first part of the compound verb. Usually. So it would be "He has always..." and "She will frequently..." and "That train has habitually..."

But it's a rough rule, and it was followed out the window here:

> As he has labored to fill his outsized war chest, the governor has, like everyone else, had to endure his share of negative publicity.

And again here:

> ...Jennings had, in the early 1980's, ushered in the era of the television news anchor...

Splitting "has" from "had," and "had" from "ushered," is downright ugly. Make it natural: "...the governor, like everyone else, has had to..." and "Jennings, in the early 1980's, had ushered in..."

# Adverb, Start of Sentence

## *Comfortable "ly"*

Notwithstanding prejudice against "hopefully," and some other frowning, adverbs work perfectly well at the beginnings of sentences (and clauses) and are usually preferable to adjectives in those environs.

*See Important/Importantly.*

# Adverse/Averse

## *Adverse Effect*

> Big companies are adverse to publicity — and the bigger the company, the more adverse.

N ope. "Adverse" means "negative" or "bad"; we wouldn't say the companies were "bad to publicity." The writer meant they were opposed to it, uneasy about it, and the word he wanted was "averse." A few paragraphs later, the text spoke of "heavy adverse publicity," and that was just right. ADverse, as in bAD.

# Adviser/Advisor; Historic/Historical

## *Distinctions and Differences*

S ome distinctions between similar words need to be maintained because they're useful; examples abound in this fount of wisdom. Here's another: the distinction between "historic" and "historical."

In the phrase "Chile, Bolivia's historic enemy," the choice was unfortunate. By hoary consensus, "historic" has been reserved for events of great moment, like the Battle of Yorktown or the Emancipation Proclamation. To describe a longtime pattern, like Chilean–Bolivian enmity, or for any variation on the broad notion "relating to history," the job is best done by "historical." Different words for different meanings. Useful.

Not at all useful is the insistence among the finicky (including this traveler at one time) that "advisor" is a misspelling, an ignorant back-formation from "advisory," and that only "adviser" is correct. "Advisor" is everywhere, and it was not surprising to find "became a valued advisor" in a historical (not historic) work of impeccable pedigree. So we should pick a spelling — flipping a coin will do — stay with it, and relax.

# Affect/Effect

## *Think 'A'...or 'E'*

Mark Stevens, director of public information for the Denver Public Schools, e-mailed to ask about a fairly widespread mental block: "I could use a neat way to remember the correct use for 'affect' and 'effect.'" Here's an attempt at a formula to help keep them separate.

"Affect," except for the specialists mentioned below, is a verb, meaning to cause change in something: His headache affected his ability to concentrate. Verbs are words of action. So think "A" — Affect, Action — something is Acting on something else.

"Effect" is usually a noun, a word for a thing, in this case a result of something: Aspirin had the desired effect, and he passed the exam. Think "E" for End product or Eventuality.

So much for the most common situations.

A less common (but useful) form of "effect" is a verb meaning to bring about or cause to happen: She effected a revolution with her challenge to the grading system.

A nuanced (and useful) form of "affect" is a verb meaning to move, emotionally: The scene affected her greatly; it was a profoundly affecting moment.

And in the social sciences, alas, "affect" can be a noun, meaning a feeling or emotion as shown or described by a patient. But we can leave that one to the social scientists.

(Rosalind Warfield-Brown, a teacher at Hampden-Sydney College in Virginia and a freelance editor, suggested a word to help people get around that mental block: VANE. That's Verb = Affect / Noun = Effect. That certainly works for the two basic meanings.)

# After/Following

See Before/Prior To

# Allude/Refer

## *Indirect and Direct*

A newspaper article misused a word when it reported that a shadowy character was "known as Abu al-Janna, or 'the Father of Heaven,' a reference to the postmortem bliss promised by the Koran to Muslims who die in jihad."

The word that missed was "reference."

To refer means to speak of something directly; to mention something indirectly is to allude. "Shakespeare wrote a lot of good stuff" is a *reference* to Shakespeare. But "As somebody once said, 'To be or not to be,'" is not a *reference* to Shakespeare, it's an *allusion*.

And the phrase "Father of Heaven" was an allusion. It did not directly mention the Koran or its promises.

"Allude," which some people seem to use to show off, is usually the problem, and it's not always obvious which word is the right one.

A report about campaigning in Germany probably had it right when it said one candidate "alluded" to his opposition to the Iraq war. No specific mention of the war occurred in several quotations from the candidate, but he did speak of his willingness to criticize "big partners."

But here, given the specifics, it sure seemed that the company "referred":

> In a recent earnings report, the company alluded to plans to "exit even more underperforming markets."

And when a baseball color commentator says very clearly, "Pinch-hitting is tough," and his play-by-play partner says "Pinch-hitting, which you alluded to," that's word abuse.

# Along With

### *Getting Along*

> Mr. Lott, along with Speaker Newt Gingrich, were among those who signed the letter to the F.C.C.

The phrase between commas is one of those parenthetical distractions that life serves up. The subject of the sentence remains "Mr. Lott," so we have to say "was among those."

The same trap opens with "as well as" and a lot of other interruptions: "The Mayor will now have an opportunity to demonstrate…that it is his management techniques, not any one person, that is responsible for the drop in crime."

"Not any one person" distracted the writer (and editor) into thinking that the subject of the last clause of the sentence had become singular. But the subject is still "techniques," so the clause should read "that are responsible…" We can avoid the traps by watching out for whatever just goes along for the ride.

# Alternate/Alternative

### *Alternating Current?*

The article said a utility "plans to freeze its electric rates for five years, and by 2003 will allow all its customers to buy power from alternate sources." The writer almost certainly wanted "alternative," meaning providing a choice among options.

"Alternate" means by turns, or every other, as in "alternate Sundays." (Custom has also allowed "alternate" referring to choice or substitution in such expressions as "alternate juror" or "Alternate Route 22." Irritating, but there it is.)

# Antecedents

### *Remembering Those Gone Before*

Everybody knows that a pronoun needs to agree with its antecedent, the earlier noun that the pronoun stands in for. We can't, for instance, say "Democrats" and follow up with "it."

But the problem is trickier in sentences like this one, which are common:

> The testimony provided the strongest corroboration to date of White House claims that its office of personnel security...

The antecedent for "its" seems to be "White House," but that doesn't work. A pronoun's antecedent has to be a noun, and in that sentence, the executive mansion is used as an adjective, modifying "claims." To make it right, change it to "...the White House's..." Using the possessive turns "White House" back into a noun, and we're home free.

That's sense; for a look at some nonsense, see Possessive Nouns with Pronouns.

# As Such (Transition)

### *A Shaky Link*

Transitional words and phrases are often necessary, but not as often as we use them. The exhausted "meanwhile," the slightly haughty "indeed," the pince-nez-professorial "to be sure" sometimes arise from an unexamined reflex rather than from sense.

And sometimes when knee jerks, foot lands in mouth. It did in the unthinking reach for transition here:

> ...an independent Chronicle, with no Examiner to carry, would be much more profitable. As such, there have been rumors for more than a decade...

As such what? No word or phrase in the first sentence leads logically to "As such, there have been rumors..." in the second. And making the phrase refer to an entire sentence — in effect, to nothing identifiable — is asking it to do too much.

"As such" needs preparation, a person or thing or characteristic to which it refers, as in "Jones was a libertarian, and as such he opposed many government programs." Or "The cook was Dutch and behaved as such."

If a transition was needed in our example (whether it was is at least arguable) then "For that reason" or "Consequently," or "And so" or other things we can all imagine would have built one. "As such" was a misguided reflex; we need to stop and think.

# Assure/Ensure/Insure

## *Not a Sure Thing*

Do other languages suffer from as many words that sound like each other as English does? It's hard for us unilinguals to know, but it seems unlikely. (French has "eau" and "au" in fact, but for this memory that pretty much exhausts the subject.)

In English, one set of sound-alikes that causes confusion consists of assure, ensure, and insure. There are guidelines, more or less useful, but the boundaries are nothing if not elastic.

"Assure" means to promise, to remove doubt, and it tends to involve an exchange between people; one person (or entity) assures another. These worked:

…so he could assure the country of the importance of the war

The victory…left the Bengals, at 9–3, assured of their first winning record since 1990.

"Ensure" means to make (something) certain; often that means certain to happen. These worked:

…judicial review to ensure that those rules have in fact been honored

Graduate assistants were retained to ensure some continuity.

The next one didn't work, though, because somebody chose the verb unwisely:

The Senate proposal…allocates money by risk only after all states are ensured funds.

That wanted to be "assured funds," or more comfortably, "assured of funds."

Yet sometimes "assure" seems to trespass —

Problems in assuring that all defendants had counsel …

— but in fact both "assure" and "ensure" work in constructions leading to a "that" clause.

"Insure" works with such constructions, too, and despite recommendations that it be restricted to financial arrangements — insurance — it wanders, especially into territory involving preparation for eventualities, where "ensure" is also natural:

take action to insure safe passage along this already undersized thoroughfare

"Insure" is also the most comfortable of the three verbs with "against," financially and more generally:

… the best way to insure against the rise of worrisome groups …

Mr. Ciampi wanted Mr. Berlusconi's commitment in writing to insure against any further misunderstandings.

Contractors...are buying up stock...to insure themselves against future price spikes.

Flexible? Oh yes. Tidy? No.

# As, Followed by ... As

### *What's Better than 'Than'?*

Words to live by: When we start a comparison with "as," we have to stay with "as." We shouldn't, for instance, write "Americans can pay twice *as* much for drugs in the United States *than* people pay in Canada."

Maybe "for drugs in the United States" was a fatal distraction. No one (hmm?) would say "twice *as* much *than* people pay." Nature and sense (not to mention the rules of syntax) require "*as* much... *as* people pay."

With no serious distraction, things nonetheless went similarly awry in a report about the apparent effect of gas exploration on a species of wild birds in the rural West.

Describing the birds' courtship areas near the gas wells, the passage said that "four times as many are inactive than active." Nature and sense again: "*as* many are inactive *as* active." And to be balanced and smooth, we can add a syllable: "as *are* active."

# As vs. So

### *As Long as It's Clear*

Amy Carlile of the Washington newspaper *Roll Call* (see Troopers/Troupers) e-mailed about a rule she remembered from somewhere that didn't seem too helpful. It called for "as" in positive comparisons and "so" in negative ones.

Comparisons weren't what Mrs. Carlile was interested in, as it happened. But the guidance is only partly sensible anyway, and only for the easy part. It's just about impossible to use "so" in a standard positive comparison; who would say Dick is *so* smart as Jane?

As for negative situations — Dick is not [as or so] smart as Jane — any insistence on "so" is an arbitrary and unnecessary addition to our burdens. We ought to feel free to use whichever word comes to mind first.

The example Mrs. Carlile was contemplating involved another kind of phrase presenting the as/so choice, where the phrase means "provided":

...so long as the nominee can secure 50 votes

Here, too, no problemo. "So long as" is fine. "As long as" is fine, too.

# As Well As, Too (Starting Sentence)

### *Starting Well*

Robyn Packard, based in Toronto as marketing editor for the international business law firm Torys LLP, asked in an e-mail, "How do you feel about using 'As well' at the beginning of a sentence?"

Not well. That phrase, in that place, doesn't violate any rule of grammar or usage. But it's unnatural and seems terribly affected — pinky-in-the-air stuff, or some writing teacher's half-baked idea of originality. Much the same could be said of "too" at the start of a sentence, where it crops up occasionally.

With perfectly idiomatic words and phrases like "in addition," "besides," "furthermore," "moreover," "also," and good old reliable "and" available to us, we don't need to hold up a sign to let everybody know we're cute.

# AttorneyS General, etc.

### *No Generals Here*

The story said a judge "at a minimum will request briefs from the Justice Department, state attorney generals and Microsoft." And an editorialist wrote of "officials who now hide behind their subordinates and inspector generals…"

But when we start with one attorney general or one inspector general and add more, it isn't generals who increase, it's attorneys and inspectors. "General" in each case is an adjective, not a noun. The correct plurals are "attorneys general" and "inspectors general" (and adjutants general).

The plurals come out wrong pretty often, especially in speech (including that of attorneys general). And some dictionaries have knuckled under, telling us it's okay either way. It's not, any more than it is, say, with sergeants major or brothers-in-law. With all such, logic limits the choice of plurals to one.

# *The* Authorities

### *Experts or Cops?*

The sentence spoke of "actions which authorities charge ultimately led to Officer Guidice's death." For clarity's sake, and to preserve a nicety of the language, we should usually save "authorities" for people with great knowledge in their fields — experts. The law-enforcement types are better described as "*the* authorities." (In the example, a widely observed rule would put a comma after "which" and another after "charge," or maybe just substitute "that" for "which." See That/Which.)

# Award/Reward

### *It's All in the Giving*

K irk Arnott, an assistant managing editor of the *Columbus Dispatch* in Ohio, e-mailed to ask whether there was a succinct way of remembering the difference between "award" and "reward." He'd been irked when he read that a proposal for a different way of determining the professional hockey standings "would reward three points for a regulation win instead of the current two."

Both words involve giving. "Award" is used for the thing given: The hockey system gives — awards — three points; the points are awarded.

"Reward" applies to the person or entity that receives something: the system gives to — rewards — teams; the teams are rewarded.

Thinking "a" ought to help. "Award" is interchangeable in such contexts with allocate, allot, and assign. The system would allocate, allot, assign — or award — three points.

On the "r" side, we can remember that it's the recipient who is rewarded.

# Awhile/A While

### *Same Difference*

D avid Cohn, working at the time as an intern at the *Columbia Journalism Review*, asked a question a lot of us never think to ask: What's the difference between "awhile" and "a while"?

One answer is that the difference is a pure nuisance, of no value whatever, since the underlying meanings are identical. Be that as it may, "awhile," one word (and one we could do without) means "for a period of time." We are supposed to use it adverbially, to describe the action of a verb, as we would use (say) the adverb "slowly": walk slowly; walk awhile.

The two words "a while" mean "a period of time" and constitute a noun phrase. We are supposed to use a preposition in front of it: Walk for a while; I'll be there after a while. Two words are also recommended for "a while ago," "a while back," and such like, though why is anybody's guess.

There it is, for what it's worth. In practice, all such guidance is ignored as often as it's followed, and the sun still rises every morning. This one is a strong candidate for first on the all-time list of things not worth worrying about.

# Bacterium/Bacteria

### *One Bug, Two Bugs...*

B axter Omohundro of Columbus, Ga., a retired Knight Ridder editor, read the discussion of "Media, Plural" (which see), sent an amen by e-mail, then added,

> My list of abused words is long, but the next time you feel like leaping to the defense of an increasingly neglected singular, I would nominate "bacterium" — "This bacteria is..." Ugh!

Ugh works.

*See also Criterion/Criteria, Phenomenon/Phenomena; Grafitto/ Grafitti; Media*

# (Feel) Bad/Badly

## *Two Ways, with Feeling*

A visitor to the Web site said she and her boyfriend differed over the phrase "I feel badly." He insisted it was the right way to describe sadness. She held that "badly," an adverb, describing how something is done, can't be used where an adjective, describing a thing or condition, is called for; it had to be "I feel bad." In fact, an ancient joke among people who hate "feel badly" is that it can only mean to suffer from an underdeveloped sense of touch. But we can have it both ways. (And some of us feel strongly about that.)

Used to describe an emotional state, "feel badly" is widely accepted by good writers and editors and is perfectly natural. It's an exception to the rule governing linking (copulative) verbs — be, become, seem, feel, grow, look — which generally require adjectives. To describe an upset stomach, though, "feel badly" sounds less natural, but it has some scholarly support.

And wherever the pain arises, "feel bad" is technically unassailable, always safe.

(It's tempting to note Ulysses S. Grant's observation in his *Memoirs* that two comrades "felt badly over this estrangement." But that would not only be inconclusive for this argument, it would also require, in fairness, acknowledging that Grant at one point wrote of a time "prior to the first call for volunteers." Seeming to endorse the dread "prior to" [which see] is too much to ask.)

# Baited/Bated (Breath)

## *Anyone for a Mint?*

What sort of enticement do we have here — cheese? worms?

...as manufacturers wait with baited breath...

The "i" is misplaced, of course, in "baited breath," and it's a fairly frequent intruder.

The word "bate," a shaved-down form of "abate," means to moderate or restrain. The expression "with bated breath" means anxiously, tensely.

And except for that expression, "bate" barely exists in our day.

# Because/Since

## *Since You Asked...*

André E. Maillho, managing editor of *Gambit*, an alternative weekly in New Orleans, noticed that

You, like millions of other Americans, tend to use the word "since" to convey a causative relationship...An old editor once scolded me to differentiate between "since" and "because" and it's been a reflex ever since...What's your take?

That old editor once had a fairly numerous following, but the words are usually interchangeable. A problem can arise — maybe the reason for the old editor's edict — if "since" can be read mistakenly in its time sense: "Since she called him a fool, he has stopped campaigning" is ambiguous, for example. When there's no trap of that kind, "since" means "because" and vice versa.

# Before/Prior To

See Prior To/Before

# Beg the Question

## *Tricky Beggar*

A painful topic long evaded in Language Corner finally seemed unavoidable after a note arrived from Amy Carlile, deputy managing editor of *Roll Call*, a Washington weekly that covers Congress: What does "beg the question" *really* mean?

The term comes from formal debating and denotes the classic fallacy in logic of proving a point using a premise that has not, itself, been proven. (In law, a commonly heard objection to such maneuvers is "assumes a fact not in evidence.")

One form of begging the question is circular argument — basing two conclusions on each other, A proving A: The editor must be right because editors don't make mistakes.

But the begging needn't be circular; A, unproven, can be used to prove B. Way back when, H. W. Fowler cited the proposition, "That fox hunting is not cruel, since the fox enjoys the fun." There is no proof, of course, of the fox's state of mind.

In our time the phrase has become popularly understood — it apparently sounds good to a lot of people — to mean to duck a question, or to raise or imply a question that cries out for an answer. For example (among thousands), a pundit on the American presence in Iraq: "It then begs the question, if we're going to stay the course, what's the course?"

We don't need "beg the question" for such meanings, and it's sometimes useful in its original sense. Whether that sense will ever again prevail seems, at best, debatable.

# Beside/Besides

## *Nearby or Something More?*

"There was plenty to do beside wait and worry," the article said, and the problem may have been only a typographical error. But just in case, "beside," by widespread agreement, means "next to," "at the side of."

"Besides," with an "s," is a short, natural word for "in addition to" or "as well as": There were 10 players besides Joe; besides losing the game, Joe broke a leg.

Thus, "there was plenty to do besides wait and worry."

# Between/Among

## *Among You, Me, and the Lamppost?*

A reader was kind enough to write to applaud our sermon on "unique," but he also had a complaint.

A nearby article in that issue of the *Columbia Journalism Review*, he noted in an e-mail, said,

> And their success will depend largely on cooperation — between the media and the court and, especially, BETWEEN members of the press [reader's emphasis].

> "Since 'members' is plural," the note asked, "should it not read 'among members of the press'"?

Probably not. The rule that calls for "among" when more than two things are being discussed is a rule of thumb, and a coarse one. In any group, the members may relate to each other in a block or, as seems more likely in the reader's example, individually — A to B, A to C, B to A, and so on. So "between members of the press" seems more sensible, though "among" isn't technically wrong.

"Between" was also wanted in this passage from a newspaper report:

> The F.B.I.'s refusal of the White House's request was a vivid example of the tensions among the White House, the Justice Department and the F.B.I.

As the article made clear, the tensions arose between the White House and the Justice Department, between the Justice Department and the F.B.I., and between the White House and the F.B.I.

And for this one, you didn't need the context to know that the writer (or, at least as likely, the editor) was following a rule of thumb out the window:

> ...an airline charter service that operates among Havana, the Bahamas and Mexico.

Those planes obviously fly *between* Havana and the Bahamas, to mention only one leg of their travels.

The rule of thumb is often the one to follow, of course, as it was when the announcer said the officials at a basketball game had "49 years' experience between the three." The *total* of experience was the whole group's, and the word had to be "among."

# 'Between...and,' Not 'Between...to'

## *That Space Is an 'And'*

John Luke, a freelance writer and editor in Sierra Madre, Calif., sent this complaint:

> For years, I've been grinding my teeth when radio journalists say things like "between seventy to eighty people were seen sliding down the rope." I want to respond by telling them they're putting me between a rock to a hard place. You don't

see this in print much, but it's all over radio news, even on the high-quality stations.

Actually, it happens in print, too; from a newspaper front page:

> ...stole design information about America's most advanced warhead, the W-88, between 1984 to 1988.

Mr. Luke is right, of course — "between" in such places takes "and," not "to." And the people who make him grind his teeth belong where they've been putting him.

# Between/In Between

See In, Up, On

# Between the Cracks

## *Cracks to Fill*

Alex McKale (see "Hitting Milestones") e-mailed to say,

> Another phrase I've heard misused too frequently is "between the cracks." The speaker generally means "through the cracks" or "in the cracks."

Quite so. It's another phrase that turns intended meaning on its head (see Could/Couldn't Care Less).

The writer who suggested using a creeper "to plant in between the cracks of paving stones on a terrace" obviously wasn't thinking of some killer plant that would punch its way through those stones, yet it was the stones that were "in between the cracks." Something was wanted to fill the space either *between* the stones or *in* the cracks.

The same logic applies in figurative use. If certain insurance policies "have often fallen between the regulatory cracks," they haven't escaped bureaucratic attention, which is what the writer had in mind. They've landed in plain view on solid ground. They would enter the void only by falling *through* the cracks or *into* them.

# Bid,Bid,Bade

### *Do Not Hasten to Bid*

The picture showed a uniformed man hugging a woman, and the caption said he "bid farewell to his wife." One way or another, "bid" wasn't a great choice.

If the publication's caption style required the present tense, "bids" was the word. If style wanted past tense, the choice was "bade."

"Bid" is an unusual verb in that its past tense and participle vary with context. For financial matters, and in the sense of "try," both those tenses — along with the present tense — use "bid": at the auction, she bid on the painting; he bid for a role in the production; the company had bid on the contract. "Bid" is also the choice all around for what bridge players do.

And some prefer "bid" for all occasions. But for greetings and partings and commands, "bade" is the preferable past tense, and the participle is either "bade" or, preferably, "bidden" — the prime minister bade the president welcome; they bade us adieu; by then she had bidden him go and never darken her door again.

Much the same guidance can be applied to "forbid/forbade," though that verb takes an infinitive with "to" (she forbade him to go) or a direct object (she forbade his lecture). The participle is "forbidden."

Maintaining profoundly artificial differences like those between "more than" and "over" (which see) is silly. Preserving the age-old difference between "bid" and "bade" is nice, somehow — modestly, forgivably erudite.

# 'Big of a'

## *Of Idiom*

W arren Corbett, a writer and editor in Bethesda, Md., e-mailed about an annoying trend:

> At some point the phrase "not that big a deal" became "not that big of a deal." I see it frequently. It grates on me, but I cannot articulate the distinction between "not that big of a deal," wrong in my eyes, and "not that much of a problem," obviously correct. If I'm not making too big a deal of it, please help.

The answer seems to lie largely with idiom — the way things are expressed simply because they're expressed that way. But maybe there's logic involved, too. In "not that much of a problem," "much" is working as a noun. Using "of" with it seems natural, as it is, say, with "sort of a" and "kind of a" (when followed by singular nouns).

But with an adjective, in this case "big," the "of" seems unnatural and unidiomatic — certainly redundant, and for some of us illiterate.

Nor should the distaste be confined to phrases using "big." If anything, the bigger the adjective the more grating, as when the basketball announcer exclaimed how welcome it was "to have this exciting of a game."

*Merriam-Webster's Dictionary of English Usage,* under "of a," says that in phrases like "that big of a deal," the usage is relatively recent, oral American idiom, rare in print except in reported speech.

May it remain rare in print. And if people stop speaking that way, that will be fine, too.

But Mr. Corbett remains concerned. "Idiom is defined by usage," he notes, "so 'not that big of a deal' is likely to become accepted."

If so, maybe not that big a deal. Definitely grating, though.

# Borne Out, with an 'E'

## *Born to Be Borne, or Vice Versa*

The mix-up is fairly common:

> Such reports seem born out by help-wanted advertising...

The correct spelling is "borne," with an "e." It's one of two participles of the verb "bear," which can mean give birth (past tense "bore," participle "born") or carry (past tense and participle "borne").

The participle without the "e" is used for actual or figurative birth: a star is born, to a born loser; things are born of necessity or desperation; children are born in or out of wedlock. For everything else, including the cited form "bear out," meaning to prove or confirm, add the "e." The star was borne for nine months by her hard-working mother, and then was born.

This was just exactly wrong:

> But the brunt of the evening's jokes were born by the President and the other major impeachment figures...

Our word has nothing to do with birth; it has to do with carrying (a burden). The choice had to be "borne." (And incidentally, shouldn't the little verb be "was"? All the jokes weren't borne by the president, only the brunt of them; should "jokes" take command of the sentence? Here's a no vote, though it's a close call; see Collective Nouns.)

And finally, some people, an article said, "harbor anti-Semitic attitudes borne of years of conflict." The writer and editor didn't want that "e"; those attitudes were born of — they arose from, were given birth to by — those years of conflict. (The immortal H. W. Fowler's analogous citation was "The melancholy born of solitude.")

# Both

## *Putting Two Together*

The word "both" takes two elements and makes them one. With that in mind, consider this:

> Both of the candidates tried to link their opponent to the perceived weaknesses of their parties.

Their opponent? The two of them, together, have an opponent? Not what the writer meant; he meant, "Each of the candidates tried to link his opponent to the perceived weakness of his party." (Or, for total clarity, "...the opponent's party.")

One news article had it both ways. Near the beginning, "Both sides remain far apart in those discussions" was wrong; the two, together, weren't far apart from something else or some other things. Near the end, "But the lawyers said the two sides were still far apart on several fronts" got it right.

# Brackets

## *The Bracket Blues*

Except when excerpting text or in such devices as blurbs and pull-quotes, bracketing material inside quotations is, not to put too fine a point on it, an abomination.

- Genuinely good quotes are mangled by bracketing: "Our prisons are full of [those who were] abused children," he said. Clunk. The story had already set up the quote adequately, but even if it hadn't, a phrase before the quote, not that awful hiccup inside it, was the solution. (Explanations can also come after quotes, of course; the point here is that hitting the reader over the head with a hammer is unkind.)

- Bracketing can puzzle readers and even make them suspicious (what did that guy *really* say?): "I read about teams getting competitive [by signing] other players," he said. Anyone's guess.
- Bracketing assaults the ear, making for agonizing reading: "'No one among the big three [networks] would run this long at the top [the beginning of the show] with these kinds of stories' now, Rather said." In a word, aargh. If a quote needs that much help (this one didn't) why bother to quote at all?
- Some bracketing results in ridiculous baggage inside quotation marks: "They started calling me Duke because I wear No. 4 [Duke Snider's old number]," said Piercy. Just end the quoted matter at "4" and *tell* the rest.

Most importantly, bracketing is lazy — a kind of stenography. In that regard it's a soulmate of that other hallmark of bad journalistic writing, the breathless stringing-together of words before a name (see False Titles). Both are abdications of our duty to write English sentences. On deadline? No time to write? Try. It could become a habit.

This, however, was absolutely not the way to handle the problem:

> If I'd had a walkie-talkie, I'd have told jockey Victor Espinoza to pull him up.

Real people do not say in conversation, and trainers do not respond to shouted questions after a big-time horse race, "I'd have told jockey Victor Espinoza" — using the first name along with the job description. It just doesn't happen, and it didn't. A Nexis search showed slight variations in different accounts of the postrace analysis. Some of the many versions had just "Victor," others just "him." Others put brackets around "jockey" or "Espinoza" or, heaven help us, both. But "jockey Victor Espinoza" seems to have been a singular contortion.

Presumably a writer or an editor was loath to use brackets to provide the name or names missing from the real quotation. It's good to be loath that way. But it was possible to work around the problem, as it almost always is. Working the jockey's name into the text before using the quote, then quoting accurately — as some reports clearly did — is a wonderfully natural solution. But even brackets are better than phrasing so tortured its falsity jumps off the page.

# Broadcast, the Verb

## *Keep It Simple*

The literate choice for past tense and participle is "broadcast" — no "ed" on the end. See "Lightening"; "Forecasted."

# Brothers-in-Law, etc.

See AttorneyS General, etc.

# Call Up

See In, Up, On

# Cardinal/Ordinal Numbers

## *Cardinal Rules*

A Little League team's players, the article said, "picked up their third World Series victory in as many days."

There's a common affectation there, and it doesn't track. As many as what? As many as third? No, obviously.

"Third" is an ordinal number, denoting the position of something in a sequence. "As many as" needs to refer to a quantity, not a position, and that requires a cardinal number — here, "three."

If the sentence had said "picked up three World Series victories in as many days," that would have been fine. But for all that, "as many as" is a little forced and shopworn. What's wrong with "their third World Series victory in three days"?

# Cast, the Verb

### *Leave It Alone*

Like its relatives "broadcast" and "forecast," it takes a plain past tense and participle — "cast," with no "ed." See also "Lightening"; "Forecasted."

# Center Around/On

### *Caught in the Middle*

An e-mail visitor from Canada (where "center" is spelled with "re" at the end) sought an opinion about the phrase "centered around" and offered his own:

> I have long believed that the phrase "centred around" was logically impossible and that the preferred form is "centred on."

Database searches suggest that the "on" version is in fact preferred by most people, and some commentators prescribe it. It's perfectly logical and it's unassailable. Whether "centered around" should be banished, though, is another matter.

Surely it's possible to have a number of people or things drawn from all points of the compass toward the center of some location, but leaving space at the center for whatever is doing the drawing. And how about circular movement around a central point?

These examples seemed to evoke truer images than "on" would have done:

> The gathering centered around the pair of arm-wrestling tables.
>
> ...day camps centered around San Joaquin Valley lakes and waterways...
>
> Movements of the dance are centered around the belly.

But in this example "on" would have worked better:

> ...a wide range of questions, many of which centered around how to change course in Iraq...

(It would be a rush to judgment, however, to conclude that "on" should be the choice for all figurative uses; case by case.)

Idiom, which evolves, has clearly embraced both "around" and "on," along with other prepositions less commonly enlisted (about, at, in) as fit companions for "center."

# Chair/Chairperson

## *P.C. as Pain*

Political correctness has its place when the alternative is clearly bigoted; the old default "he," for example (see He or She, etc.) just isn't acceptable. And despite some last-gasp defenders, "chairman" as an automatic default choice isn't acceptable, either.

But to call a person a "chair" is so graceless it hurts; the p.c. is as gentle as a jackhammer.

In contexts involving legislative and other more or less orderly proceedings, of course, "chair" has been firmly established for ages — rulings by the chair and appeals to the chair abound. But those seem to involve a place where somebody sits, more than the someone sitting.

But a "chair's to-do list"? A plan to "pick a new state chair"? A list of "chairs" busy at myriad tasks? Goodness, he shouted. Grace, he pleaded.

If the sex of a person occupying such a position is known, it's perfectly natural to use "chairman" or "chairwoman." Why, then, 19 "chairs" in a single published list of people's names? That's not only p.c., it's mindless.

The story that mentioned the "chair's to-do list" was trickier. The topic was the burdens borne by people, mostly referred to only generically, who head committees that put on worthy-cause events. "Chair" or a variation (e.g., chairing, co-chair) appeared 8 times in a little over 300 words.

"Head," "director," "leader," and "chief" were available, as was "coordinator," a label the writer mentioned but abandoned.

But when there's a vacancy at the top of the English department, how do we advertise for someone to fill the job? How write journalistically about the search?

No contrivance we might come up with would fool a soul on campus. All have been conditioned, in roughly a single generation, to call the person in charge of just about anything a "chair" (or increasingly, the even uglier "chairperson") with or without an identity attached.

And sadly, the infection has spread from academe through realms public and private across the English-speaking world.

So, these suggestions:

- Never call a named person a piece of furniture; Dick is a chairman, and Jane is a chairwoman.
- Avoid "chair" in generic contexts when humanly possible.
- If all else fails — but only then — swallow hard and write "chair."

# Cohort

## *Quantity and Quality*

Some thoughts in this collection about "decimate" (which see) reminded Eric Rawlins, a retired programmer living in Berkeley, Calif., of another frequently abused word rooted in the military of ancient Rome: cohort.

The word first designated a Roman army unit of several hundred men. It came to be used — increasingly as cohorts, plural — to mean any military group, and eventually any band of companions or associates.

So far so good, or at least passable.

But the use of the word in the plural, with an "s," clearly led to the inference that "cohort," no "s," was an acceptable singular, referring to an individual person. And now some print dictionaries and at least two of the on-line kind include "a companion" and the like in their definitions of "cohort."

That's where Mr. Rawlins draws the line, and he gets no argument here. Cohort, he e-mailed, "does not mean a pal or a buddy, or any kind of individual at all (as in the ubiquitous 'he's a cohort of mine')."

At this writing a Google search shows 430 instances of "a cohort of mine." Not an overwhelming number in that universe, but the barbarians are at the gates.

We should keep trying to hurl them back. There are lots of words for "associate" and such — no need to steal another. And like "decimate" applied to a single person, "cohort," used to denote the guy at the next desk or the next bar stool, is just too much of a stretch.

# Collective

## *Don't Call Collect*

"**A**s we ponder this, as we shake our collective heads,..." the commentator intoned. Well, if it's collective, it's a single thing, "our collective head." Sounds dumb either way, though, as phrases using "collective" often do. "As we shake our heads," maybe?

The plight of a four-year-old girl found wandering in the street after her mother's murder got a lot of attention from the news folks, naturally, and one television news anchor was moved to declare that the little one had "captured the city's collective heart."

What did "collective" add to the cliché? Wood.

# Collective Nouns

## *Sensible Notion*

**T**his was awkward, to put it kindly:

Both former educators, the...couple plans to see the ballet and symphony while in Florida.

Rigidity was at work; a "couple" just has to be singular, right?

No. "Couple," like "family" and some other collective nouns, can go either way, and "couple" is usually best as a plural. Just as some superficially plural phrases sometimes have to be treated as singular, so collective nouns should be treated as plural when that makes the most sense.

The principle grammarians invoke is "notional agreement" — if the idea is plural, make the verb plural. Deciding about that can require thought, though, not just a knee jerk. Worse yet, the difference in meaning is sometimes so minute that either singular or plural works.

But in our example, even if the sentence began in the middle, without "both" and "educators" to make the error so conspicuous, "the couple plan" would be preferable. We're talking about two people, not some unit. Jane plans and Dick plans; the couple plan.

But if some disaster struck and they were really angry about it, we might say — after some thought — "the couple has filed a suit against the theater."

Some thought would have imposed logic on this passage:

> And a growing list of investors…is seeking an audience with city officials or state regulators…

There's no *list* scurrying around City Hall or the capitol seeking audiences; there are people. The notion of the sentence is clearly plural: investors *are* seeking.

*See also Fewer/Less; They Each; Tons Was*

# Compare To/With

## Weighty Prepositions

A rule was invented back in the mid-19th century, and is prescribed to this day, for using "compare." It proclaimed that "compare to" should be used when we mean to emphasize how things are alike and "compare with" when we mean to emphasize contrast.

We would compare a baboon *to* a chimpanzee, perhaps, and this year's revenues *with* last year's.

But the line between the two kinds of emphasis is often so blurry that we need a footnote to let the rule-obsessed know why we've made a particular choice of preposition.

If we started comparing those apes and got to describing their differences, would we have to go back and change "to" to "with"? What if this year's revenues were virtually unchanged from last year's?

(A purist would argue that our purpose in one case is still to liken and in the other to contrast. In a word, speaking as a reader, so what?)

The rule has no underlying logic — it's as arbitrary as they come — so it's hard to remember which preposition goes with which kind of comparison.

That's why, in practice, writers and editors seem to get the choice of preposition wrong as often as not. Happily, their lapses have no effect on human progress.

Comparing is comparing. It really doesn't matter which preposition we do it with.

# Comprise

## *The Whole and the Parts*

The story spoke of "the 30 companies whose stocks comprise the Dow Jones industrial average." It's exactly the other way around.

The stocks make up (or constitute or compose) the average. It's the average that comprises the stocks, because the whole comprises the parts.

The average (the whole) also *consists of* the stocks, *is made up of* the stocks; either of those, among others, is a more down-to-earth way than "comprise" of getting the idea across. As "comprise" has gained admirers, an aroma of pretension has wafted over from their incorrect use of it. But if we fall in love with it, let's use it right; no word should have two opposite meanings.

"Comprise" comes through French from the Latin "comprehendere," which also gave us the English word "comprehend," which is synonymous in one of its meanings — embrace, encompass — with "comprise."

And "comprise" is a near-synonym for "include," except that it means to include everything. If "include" wouldn't make sense — those stocks obviously don't *include* the Dow — we can't use "comprise."

And while we're at it, that's also why we can't use "is comprised of." Would we say "is included of"? Doesn't make sense.

# Could/Couldn't Care Less

### *It's about Caring*

Speaking of meaning turned upside down...

The article said the lawyer representing a murder victim's family made it clear that the family wasn't interested in cooperating with the media horde, "that the family could care less about exclusives." But if those people could care less, they do care some, and that's not at all what the writer meant.

The phrase has to be negative: "could not care less." That means the family cares so little — presumably not at all — that it can't reduce the caring any further.

A quick Nexis search suggests that we bat about .500 on this one, which would be great if baseball were our game.

# Criterion/Criteria, Phenomenon/Phenomena

### *Give Us an A! Give Us an...On!*

But don't mix them up, as in "The main criteria is youth, which leaves him out."

The singular of the Greek/English word is "criterion," which was needed here because only one thing — youth — was being considered. If experience, say, were added to the mix, "criteria" would be in order. It's plural, and may it always be.

And while in Greece, consider this: "The Asian market is a new phenomena..." There's only one market in that passage, so we want a singular, so we want "phenomenon."

*See also Bacterium/Bacteria; Grafitto/Grafitti; and Media*

# Curriculum(s)

See Graffito/Graffiti

# Danglers

## *Memoirs Don't Write*

This construction, called a dangler, is as common as the flowers that bloom in the spring:

> A first-time author at age 66, McCourt's memoir has topped best-seller lists and won critical acclaim.

What that says, literally, is that the memoir is a first-time author. That's because the first clause, "A...66," describes the subject of the second, and that subject is "memoir." It is the memoir, not McCourt, that "has topped."

The sentence needs to be reworked. Maybe "McCourt, a first-time author at age 66, finds his memoir atop..." Or "McCourt, etc., has written a memoir that..." However we work it out, we can't make the opus its own author.

# Decimate

## *It Takes Ten, Roughly*

The word "decimate" literally means to reduce by a tenth, from the legendary Roman practice of killing every tenth man in a mutinous or otherwise dicey military outfit on the ground that at all costs, discipline must be maintained. The word has come to mean to destroy, put out of action, or seriously damage a large part of a body of people or things: "The U.S. fleet had been decimated at Pearl Harbor" works, as does "the tree-chomping beetles that decimated Greenpoint, Brooklyn, two years ago."

But it was a considerable stretch when the eloquent elder statesman said the scandal of the day had "decimated" the president's family, which numbered three. How, then, account for the review that said a performance let a play's audience walk "right into the mind of its decimated hero"?

Applying "decimate" to an individual person or thing is more than a stretch. It makes meaningless a word with a clear and honorable pedigree.

*See also Cohort.*

# 'Declined Comment'

## *Who Offered?*

"Committee Democrats," the article reported, "declined comment until they could discuss Mr. Hyde's plan." A frequent goof, "declined comment" in this case says somebody asked, "Hey, Democrats, want some comment?" and the Democrats replied, "No thanks."

The standard English for such things involves "to": promised *to* marry me, refused *to* talk to me, planned *to* sic the dog on me, decided *to* shoot me.

Someone, some time, somewhere in journalism, thought "declined comment" was snappy, or something. Nonsense. It has never even reached the level of idiom; it's just a quirky affectation.

Make it, as generations of news folk have been (unevenly) taught, declined *to* comment.

# Defining Clause

See That/Which

# Democratic, the Adjective
## *No Taking Sides*

"Some of the Democrat ferment is positioning for the 2000 election," the analytical story said, and that was partisan (no doubt inadvertently so).

"Democrat" as an adjective is relatively recent Republican coinage, designed to head off any subconscious inference that the opposition is truly "democratic." But that word is part of the party's official name, and using the shorter form — which even some Democratic politicians do in error on occasion — endorses a political position, however inadvertently.

# Difference/Differential
## *Vive la Differential?*

Steve Parrott, director of university relations at the University of Iowa (see Important/Importantly) had a legitimate gripe.

> While I appreciate that you recognize the difference between the printed and spoken word, I hope and pray that you will admonish sportscasters who use "differential" when the word

"difference" would seem to suffice for describing the score of a sporting event.

Suffice it does. And "differential" indeed has a drumbeat quality in sports broadcasts — one of those awful things some of us do when we want to sound fancy. But the abuse of "differential" is not new, or limited to one medium.

The second edition (1965) of H. W. Fowler's *Dictionary of Modern English Usage* discussed the legitimate use of the word, as noun and adjective, not to mean "difference" but to denote something *based* on a difference — differential rates of pay, for instance, varying by the skills required for a job. (Some of us remember the night differential — extra pay to compensate for the pain of working when most of our colleagues were resting from their labors.)

"But then the rot sets in," wrote the editor, Sir Ernest Gowers. "*Differentials*…is increasingly used, under the influence of LOVE OF THE LONG WORD, as an imposing synonym for differences of all sorts…Perhaps the rot might be stopped if everyone were to bear in mind that Ophelia did not say *You must bear your rue with a differential*, nor did Wordsworth write *But she is in her grave, and O the differential to me*."

Heavenly. And when the Knicks lead the Spurs 101–99, that's not a two-point differential. It's just a difference.

# Different From/Than

### *All the Differents*

All else being equal, "different from" is preferable to "different than."

An element of logic, having to do with the positive and comparative degrees of adjectives, supports the preference. But the main reason for using "different from" is that in straightforward statements — "Dick is different from Jane" — almost everyone is more comfortable with it and most modern authorities insist on it. The headline "A Monday Night Game Different Than All the Others" followed the basic form, and as a result the use of "than" was conspicuously unhappy.

Some commentators insist that we shouldn't use "than" under any circumstances, but it has fairly broad support for many situations. "Than" has been used as long as "from," after all (the British still seem fond of "different to" as well), and struggling to avoid it can lead to tortured phrasing and blown deadlines.

One pretty widely endorsed exception to the "from" rule arises when "different" is followed by a clause, a passage with its own subject and verb — something like "Architects draw for different reasons than artists do." That could be reworked to "...different reasons from the ones that inspire artists," or some such, but it would be like going around the block to reach the house next door.

"A different sort of mandate than in Iraq," by contrast, could economically and naturally have morphed into "...from the one in Iraq."

# Double Possessive I

## *Possessed, but Only Once*

"**H**is best glove work," the sports story said, "is equal to that of Ozzie Smith's." Nah. We don't need two possessives. "That of" is a possessive, and so is "Smith's." Make it "equal to that of Ozzie Smith" or "equal to Ozzie Smith's."

*See also Oddities ("A friend of mine")*

# Double Possessive II

## *Overly Possessive?*

**W**hat to do about situations like "China and South Korea's rise to challenge Japan's position..."?

That's how it was printed, and that's one solution: With a string of possessive nouns, attach the apostrophe and the "s" only to the last one, and assume the reader will understand the earlier ones as possessive, too.

But with anything more complicated than "Dick and Jane's house," that approach is hardly a bull's-eye. It can be quite tough to follow, as in the following:

> Dr. Hwang and his team's production of stem cells...was considered...

And this was the opposite approach to the general problem:

> ...Mr. Abramoff's and Mr. Scanlon's Indian clients...

But that's a bit cluttered, and with a longer series would be more than a bit.

The optimum solution is to get the possessive notion out of the way first: "The rise of China and South Korea..."; "The production of stem cells by Dr. Hwang and his team...was considered"; "The Indian clients of Mr. Abramoff and Mr. Scanlon."

Much closer to a bull's-eye.

# Drag/Drug

## *The Drug Problem*

Just in case the children were listening when the politician — maybe funnin,' maybe not — said, "They have drug my name through the mud for two years," the past tense and participle of "drag" is "dragged." Using "drug" that way is not unheard of, but it is illiterate — here, there, and everywhere.

# Due To

## *Making Due*

O ne synonym for "due" is "attributable," and that was the idea
the writer had in mind in this sentence: "The last such blip
occurred in 1990 due to fears that the Gulf War would cut oil sup-
plies." But we wouldn't say the "blip occurred attributable to fears,"
would we? The writer wanted "because of" or "as a result of."

With "due to," some form of the verb "to be" or of other linking
verbs is usually needed. "The power failure was due to a lightning
strike" would be okay. So would "Their exhaustion seemed due
to the humidity rather than the heat." Or, for fans of the polysyl-
labic, attributable to it.

# Each Other/One Another

## *To Each His Other*

R onnie Matthew, a sub-editor at the *Times of India* living in
Ahmedabad, in the state of Gujarat, e-mailed this:

> What's the difference, in usage, between "each other" and "one
> another"? Is "each other" used in the case of two people and "one
> another" in the case of more than two?

Yes and no. There's a rule to that effect, and it's clearly arbitrary;
examine the words and it's impossible to see why any distinction is
made between the phrases. Designating "each other" for two and
"one another" for more than two was the brainstorm of an obscure
grammarian in the late eighteenth century; the phrases had been
used interchangeably for centuries before and have been since, by
writers from Samuel Johnson to Noah Webster to E. L. Doctorow.

*Merriam-Webster's Dictionary of English Usage,* the source for
that history, says the rule was "cut out of the whole cloth" and
"there is no sin in its violation." H. W. Fowler declared that "the

differentiation is neither of present utility nor based on historical usage," and the 1990s reworking of his classic *Dictionary of Modern English Usage* concludes that belief in the rule "is untenable."

*However*: Although a needless complication, the supposed rule is prescribed as style — the sometimes arbitrary dicta that publications issue in the service of consistency — by such broadly influential (and of course sensible) outfits as the Associated Press and the *New York Times*. So even though logic doesn't sanctify it, safety may.

# Echo

See Elegant Variation; Echo

# Eke

## *Every Little Bit*

When some of us who are older were younger, we were told that "eke" — almost invariably in "eke out" — should be used only to mean to augment, to make a little something last by adding a little to it or by consuming it very carefully. A standard application: a young man "working as a stevedore on the docks of Manhattan to eke out the family income." A close relative, meaning to squeeze dry: the musician who "eked out all that the instrument could deliver."

Those meanings are still perfectly legitimate, but they've been swamped by others; "eke" is a popular imp. By far the standard meaning nowadays is to just barely manage, as in "eke out a living" and its variations:

An estimated 500,000 families eke out a living...

...local businesses have been able to eke out an existence.

A common application in sports that has spread farther afield means to win narrowly:

Despite finding a way to eke out another tight victory...

In 1982, he eked out a victory in a four-way primary contest...

And then there are the odd ones: a building whose construction has been "eked out over 30 years"; the disabled man who "ekes along on $1,000 a month"; the politician who "may eke out a settlement."

Imaginative, those three, and evidence of the broad appeal of "eke." Copy them at your own risk.

# Elegant Variation; Echo

## *Elegant, Shmelegant*

An article mentioned "a letter that Tripp wrote *Newsweek* back in August after the Willey story first appeared," and continued, "In her missive, Tripp..." Another, after mentioning a "letter to the editor," continued, "His missive inspired a second letter to the editor..." Still another reported on "...a pointed, important May 8 letter to Dombeck. The missive also was signed..."

"Missive," meaning a communication, is often a stilted word. It has its uses (usually humorous), but none of our examples seems to qualify. Each simply substitutes the word for the innocuous word "letter" or that old favorite "it."

And that is the writing crime of (shudder!) elegant variation: straining conspicuously to avoid totally inoffensive repetition. An ancient cliché example is "wet, white stuff" to avoid "snow." Less shopworn, but only slightly less offensive, was the caption that mentioned "beef sandwiches" and followed up with "savory treats."

In *Modern English Usage*, H. W. Fowler declared of elegant variation, "There are few literary faults so widely prevalent, and this book will not have been written in vain if the present article should heal any sufferer of his infirmity." Here's to our good health.

\* \* \*

That entry in the Web collection prompted an important observation from Charles Levinson, a freelance journalist living in Cairo:

> It seems a fine line exists between variation that is pleasing to the reader's ear and the sort of variation that is neither useful nor pleasing.

Yes. And that brings up the subject of echo — the unthinking and annoying repetition of a word: "I'd be reluctant to take on the church on that issue." The repetition of "on" grates.

Echo is the irritating obverse of elegant variation. Avoiding two "ons" in the previous example is desirable. It's also easy, but that's not always the case. The writers who mentioned a letter and jumped to "missive" were trying to avoid echo, and they ended up in a worse pickle.

# Enormity

### *The Big and the Bad*

There's an undercurrent of awkwardness in the room, for the imminent enormity of the alternative-medicine industry will not just be demographic but also financial.

The writer's use of "enormity" that way — to denote only great size — is like using "fortuitous" (which see) to mean "lucky." In both cases, we're in danger of losing a nice precision.

"Enormity" should be reserved for things that are both huge *and* evil or outrageous, as in "their attempt to convey the enormity of the Holocaust." To denote sheer size, "enormousness," though a bit enormous, is available. So are immensity, vastness, and, uh, sheer size, among other words and phrases.

# Enumerate

See Remunerate/Renumerate

# Equally As

## *Let's All Be Equal, Once*

"**I**'d be equally as willing for a dentist to be drilling," Lerner and Loewe's Professor Higgins moaned, but those gentlemen had to consider meter, and they stuck in an extra word: "as."

That made a tautology. "Equally" contributes the needed idea of comparison, so "as" is a redundant repetition of the crucial thought. "As" wasn't needed in…

> …then they should be at least equally as important…

or in

> …was regarded as more important or equally as important…

or even once in

> …because they're both equally as bad and equally as evil and equally as destructive…

The phrase "just as," incidentally, doesn't offend the way "equally as" does. If we substitute "just" for "equally" in our examples, everything's idiomatic and comfy.

Another solution is to take out "equally," though that makes the little word "as" work pretty hard. Skipping "as" when "equally" is in the picture works best.

# Essential Clause

See That/Which

# 'Ever'; 'In History'

## *False Economy*

The death toll, a news article reported, marked "one of the worst terrorist attacks in Jordan." One of the worst this year? Since the first of the month? Since the dawn of time? For the reader-listener, the sentence is missing something.

By default, the omission of a time element in that passage means one of the worst ever, one of the worst in history. And the thinking that leads to that omission, and makes it necessary for readers to reason out the default intention, is not only rigid but also inconsiderate. It probably saves half a pint of ink over 10 years or so, but at far too great a cost.

Using "ever" or "in history" when dealing with one of a kind is natural and idiomatic. It may annoy some nit-picker somewhere, but it's kind to our readers, which is what we're about.

# Evoke/Invoke, Precipitate/Precipitous

## *Tripping over Latin Roots*

A news story said, "Eminent domain…is usually evoked for highways…" but the "oke" word was wrong. Make it "invoked," meaning called into play, appealed to, or cited in justification, and by extension put into effect. We may invoke, for example, our Fifth Amendment rights.

"Evoke" is from the same Latin root, "vocare" (meaning to call), so it, too, has to do with calling; "vocal" comes from the same place.

But "evoke" means to call forth or call to mind. Often, evoking something involves emotion — Ah, how wonderfully cotton candy evokes childhood! — and remembering the two "e" words may help separate the two "oke" words.

Another article mentioned the brief removal of a foreign leader from power and said the United States "precipitously endorsed the short-lived ouster."

"Precipitous" means steep, or falling rapidly, so the adverb means steeply or drastically, as with nasty declines in the stock market. The writer or editor wanted "precipitately," which describes excessive speed.

Both words come from the Latin root for "precipice" (a word that both may evoke, come to think of it). To remember the correct last syllable, it might help to think "a," as in "precipitate" and "haste" (in which the United States acted, the article intended to say).

The same mnemonic might have kept a news commentator and an army general, on television programs on successive nights, from warning against a "precipitous pullout" from Iraq.

# Facility

## *Too Facile by Half*

"Facility" is a graceful, useful word denoting ease, dexterity, fluency, and other attractive qualities, as when music is "played with impressive technical facility and panache." It can also be used to characterize concrete objects designed to make life easier: "Facilities may be limited at these smaller outposts."

But the way in which it's used most often — more and more every day, apparently — is as a substitute for other, much more precise words that describe structures, places, equipment and more. That way, it's flabby and irritating.

And it never quits: the files teem with everything from "horse facilities" (stables) to "breeding facilities" (puppy mills) to a "laundry facility" to a "hemophilia treatment facility" and a "sewer treatment facility"; to "gambling facilities" and "physical fitness facilities" and — honest — "state-of-the-art fermentation facilities." Nor do any prisons or jails remain in the English-speaking world. You know what *they* are.

The word is maddeningly convenient when we're in a rush. But really, we should try harder. A hospital is a hospital, a factory is a factory, an outhouse is an outhouse.

*See also Reference as a Verb*

# False Titles

## *Stringing It Out*

...Marlins Latin American scouting director Al Avila

...Democratic delegates to the convention Jim and Ann Roosevelt

...anti-affirmative action activist Ward Connerly's

And a real pip, from an otherwise literate journal that apparently does this kind of thing as a matter of style:

> ...says University of Southern California law professor and frequent Fox contributor Susan...

Why, for heaven's sake?

Along with lazy brackets inside quotations (see Brackets) false titles like those are an abdication of our duty to write English sentences. They're inelegant and unnatural. But they're also easy — don't *think*, just string all the adjectives and nouns in front of the name (or a common noun) and move on.

But do let's think, and honor our obligation to the language, and be clear, and let the reader catch a breath in the little pauses that commas contribute. "Al Avila, the Marlins' scouting director for Latin America" is natural. ("Latin American" presumably described his scouting assignment, not his geographic origin, though the false title means we have to guess). Also natural is "Jim and Ann Roosevelt, Democratic..." and "the decision by

Ward Connerly, the anti-affirmative action activist,..." Other arrangements would work in all three cases, and we might want "...Connerly, an..." (not "the") for someone truly obscure.

A less obvious and perhaps less egregious abuse: "Democratic New York Sen. Patrick Moynihan later joined in the fray." Well, the only real title there is "Senator." So "Senator Patrick Moynihan, a (or the) New York Democrat," is a solution. English.

And precision. Al Avila may have been "Latin American," but that wasn't the point. And if a company has more than one senior vice president (we should know), then "XYZ Co. senior vice president Joe Blow" is incomplete and misleading, quite apart from the question of grace. "Joe Blow, a senior vice president of XYZ Co." is more accurate, and easier on the ear.

Where to draw the line? The closer to standard English — as opposed to journalese — the better. And the longer the mulligan stew of modifiers, the farther we get from standard.

# Farther/Further

## *Farther? Further? Fussy?*

For some generations now (but not a great many), we've been told to use "farther" as an adjective or adverb when distance, literal or figurative, is involved, and "further" for the sense of "additional." (Out of gas, the car could go no farther; she made a further observation.) With all the things writers and editors need to remember, that ought to be a distinction not worth bothering about.

The words emerged in Old English as comparatives not for "far" but for "fore" or "forth," depending on which reference one consults. The experts seem to agree that "further" came first, with "farther" born as both words mutated, in Middle English, into comparatives for "far." The two forms were used for centuries for both distance and "additional" applications; Shakespeare used both, both ways, with no recorded loss of sleep, and fine modern writers have done the same.

But great (and much-needed) codifying of the hodgepodge of English started in the 18th century, and by the end of the 19th the dictum about "farther" for one thing and "further" for another had taken hold.

The rule enshrines a distinction without a difference. It's a rule for a rule's sake, regardless of the longer history and regardless of logic, and as such is an unnecessary burden. These ears find "further" more adaptable, but either word ought to be usable for either task, if our editors will let us go that far.

If only…Jerry Boggs, sports editor of the *Middlesboro Daily News* in Kentucky, read the previous paragraphs on the Web and then, on the wire, read this, about an injured quarterback: "Pennington will have further tests Monday."

So, Mr. Boggs asked in an e-mail, " 'Pennington will have FAR-THER tests' would also be acceptable?"

Technically and logically, yes, but in fact it's jarring; the arbitrary latter-day rule has succeeded too well, and "farther tests" pretty much defies idiom at this writing. For the "additional" sense the safer choice is likely to be "further."

And when "push the limits much farther" popped up in print, it was just fine, a reminder that when talking about distance, literal or figurative, we can still flip a coin and be sure of coming out right.

# Feud

## *Some Things Take Time*

The headline reported a judicial decision that had caused an instant, angry debate. A sub-heading, over a story about that reaction, read, "Bitter Feud over Ruling." That was too hasty.

Some dictionaries include a definition of "feud" that fits any old quarrel, but custom has long since restricted the word to the kind of nastiness that goes on for a good while, sometimes for generations. The squabble in question, as it turned out, was pretty much moot in a week or so, well short of even the minimalist requirements for a feud.

# Fewer/Less

## *The Odds Favor Less*

Ed Cassidy, chief fiscal officer for a charitable agency in Buffalo, e-mailed to ask,

> Can you enlighten me on when "less" and when "fewer"?

There's a rule, but a rough one indeed. What it says is that things counted individually are "fewer" and things counted in bulk are "less" — fewer apples, less fruit.

The rule doesn't seem as contorted in practice as the one involving "more than" and "over" (which see) but it's close. Time and again "less" is a better choice than "fewer," or certainly as good, with nouns that at first blush might seem to demand the countable treatment: less than a million dollars, less than three days, four members less than a quorum, and so on and on. Each of those plural nouns works as a single unit.

And emphatically, so did the key phrase in this classic example of a rule followed out the window:

> Dr. Crawford resigned in September, fewer than three months after the Senate confirmed him.

The topic was a single period lasting three months, not three months examined one by one; "less" was mandatory.

And it was much too literal-minded to say, as a good writer did (obviously with help from an editor) that a train was "fewer than twenty seconds away."

"Fewer" and "less" were interchangeable for hundreds of years, and to an extent they still are: the choice is often a close call or doesn't matter. But the invention of the rule in the 18th century has had a profound influence, especially in restricting the use of "less."

So whereas a good lawyer could probably get you off, it is at least a misdemeanor these days to say, "There are less pickles in the jar."

# First Annual

## *First and Natural*

A visitor to the *Columbia Journalism Review* Web site was shocked — in a good-natured way — to see this sentence there:

> He gets our first annual Katharine Graham Ethics in Journalism Award.

That was a spoof, but it evoked an old taboo. The visitor would have been much happier with a locution like this one:

> ...first in what is to be an annual...

The argument is over how to describe the beginning of a yearly whatsis.

"My ME would have killed me," the ex-journalist visitor wrote, meaning his managing editor, "for allowing a 'first annual' reference to appear in print. We learned that one in high school."

But maybe we should have left it in high school. The argument — involving one of those minuscule grains of logic people hunt out and latch onto — is that nothing can be "annual" until it happens at least twice.

That rigidity may be defensible as a fine point of law, but it contributes nothing to understanding; no one could possibly misread "first annual." The objection to it is overwhelmed by common sense.

Yet because a ban on "first annual" has cropped up in some usage guides, we get things like the fourth paragraph of this sermon, which uses eight words where two are perfect.

Unless we're stuck with a style dictate to the contrary, we ought to feel easy about using "first annual," as so many of our fellow English speakers do. It's just natural, and it will save readers' time and our own.

## Firstly

Not loveable; see Important/Importantly

## Five Times Below, 160% Less, etc.
### *Nowhere to Go but Up*

It wasn't clear in any of these examples what the writer and editor meant, because the math they used doesn't exist.

An expert, we were told, said a proposed power plant "would use 150 times less cooling water per kilowatt than neighboring older plants." Multiplying anything by a positive number like 150 can only increase the amount we're dealing with. Maybe the expert meant the new plant would use one 150th as much water. Or maybe not.

Rates of cancer from air pollution, another article said, vary widely, with New York City "four times the national average" (okay so far) and one rural county "five times below the average." If we multiply by five we don't end up "below" anything. "One fifth of the average," maybe? Why make the reader guess?

A report on a survey of news practices said tough interviewing was "down 160% over two years." But nothing can go down more than 100 percent; once it drops that far, it's gone. That one was caught in the editing, and the final phrasing omitted numbers. But reductions, decreases, and declines of more than 100 percent, which are impossible, are nonetheless reported with distressing frequency.

The confusion about percentages can extend to increases, too. We need to remember that starting with a rise of 100 percent, the numbers are a little tricky. A 100 percent increase doubles what we started with, 200 percent triples it, 300 percent quadruples it, and so on; 1,000 percent is 11 (not 10) times the original number.

# Flaunt/Flout

## *A Couple of 'F' Words*

The following word that begins with "f" was spelled right, and that's all the editor — your correspondent — noticed:

> As Tom Brokaw is sufficiently savvy to know this rule, his ostensible flaunting of it…

To flaunt is to show (something) off — she flaunted her new Porsche — and it wasn't the right word or even related to the right one. To flout, on the other hand, is to violate, defy, thumb one's nose at — he flouted the regulations daily and was never caught.

The writer, whose slip is more defensible than the editor's, of course meant Brokaw was flouting, not flaunting, the rule in question.

# Following

See Prior to/Before

# Fondle

## *Think 'Fond'*

**B**ack in another life, this collector got an angry letter from a reader of his newspaper who thought "fondle" was an ugly choice of synonym for "grope" in an article about a woman who had been sexually molested.

That seemed sensible and just; the word is built on "fond" and properly means to touch with affection, not in violation.

In some jurisdictions sexual abuse of others includes a category officially known as "fondling," so that's the only word to use for that offense. And some editors may find the word preferable to more candid descriptions when *self*-fondling, a surprisingly frequent public activity, becomes newsworthy.

Otherwise, even in a euphemism-crazy age when "issue" (which see) has come to mean everything from "topic" to "problem" to "calamity," it makes sense to avoid "fondle" in reference, for example, to the clergyman who got an adolescent boy drunk and touched him sexually, or the man who molested and traumatized a twelve-year-old girl, or the creature who the police said broke into several suburban homes and "typically touches, kisses and fondles his victims."

# Forbid

Make the past tense "forbade." See also Bid,Bid,Bade.

# 'Forecasted'

See "Lightening"; "Forecasted"

# 'Former Native'

## *Going Native*

The caption described a woman living in a New York suburb as "a former native of Kosovo," but unless she was literally born again, that can't be.

A "native" of someplace is someone who was born there, and the places where we're born never change. The woman was a native of Kosovo and always would be; she was a former resident. We can use "native" loosely, distinguishing, say, between natives and tourists, but the looseness has to be instantly apparent. "Former native" is illiterate and, alas, all too common.

# Fortuitous

## *Some Things Just Happen*

He was supposed to back up Barton, but early in camp Foels asked him to be a floater and learn all three positions. That proved fortuitous when Thomas was injured — White stepped in and filled the hole.

The clear implication is that White's learning three positions was a lucky or fortunate thing, which undoubtedly it was, but that isn't what "fortuitous" means; it means happening by chance. White's extra training didn't just happen; it was planned. And what happens fortuitously can turn out to be good or bad.

The word used the right way can mean, for example, things stumbled upon, as it did here:

Fortuitous products of poverty, such as lard-can trash receptacles and peach-basket hampers, can be the stuff that magazine layouts are made of.

Happy happenstance. But the junk that's grist for the layout artist's mill might be a pain in the neck for a landscape painter, and it would still be just as fortuitous.

A rule of thumb would be that nothing proves, becomes, or turns out to be fortuitous. It is fortuitous — a matter of chance rather than planning — the moment it happens, for good or ill.

A lovely, grim use of the word occurs in Graham Greene's *The Quiet American*. As a French jet with the novel's narrator aboard returns from a bombing mission in Vietnam, the pilot spots a small sampan on the river below and blows it to bits with machine-gun fire:

> There had been something so shocking in our sudden fortuitous choice of a prey — we had just happened to be passing, one burst only was required, there was no one to return our fire, and we were gone again, adding our little quota to the world's dead.

Whatever a pilot in such circumstances might have thought, the storyteller clearly didn't use "fortuitous" to mean "lucky."

# Forum(s)

See Graffito/Graffiti

# 'A Friend of Mine'

See Oddities

# From Whence

See Whence

# Fulsome; Problematic

### *Full of Problems*

Alan D. Gray of Montreal, a semi-retired business writer, e-mailed to ask for some thoughts on "problematic" and "fulsome."

Each of those words can mean pretty much what it looks like, and each has other meanings as well.

"Problematic" (or, unnecessarily, problematical) can mean simply presenting a problem, as in "a problematic stretch" of highway under construction. But subtler, overlapping meanings have long seemed to find favor: difficult to solve, puzzling or mysterious, open to doubt or suspicion, unsettled or worrisome: "The idea of sending drug-addicted women to prison when there is a desperate shortage of treatment for their addiction is problematic."

"Fulsome" looks like a word for full, generous, or abundant, and those meanings may be gaining in use. But the word was used for so long with a sneer — to mean excessive, insincere, sycophantic — that we'd better not use "fulsome praise" with generous intent unless the context is abundantly clear.

# Fused Participle; Off Of

### *Cut that Fuse!*

But a bad Marino pass on the Dolphins' ensuing series led to the ball deflecting off of running back Karim Abdul-Jabbar and into the hands of linebacker Corey Widmer.

But the bad pass didn't lead to the ball, which is what the sentence says, literally, and what a reader might think, momentarily. It led to the deflecting. The phrase "the ball deflecting" is what language technicians call a fused participle. It's often best to defuse it, as it were, and that's easy to do.

Make it "led to the ball's deflecting…" The possessive pulls the reader instantly to the real object of "led to." (And while in technical land, we should note that "off of" is considered a barbarism; drop the "of.")

In a glaring example, an article spoke of a research project "on the dangers of post-Communist Russia…" which is a very broad and slightly mystifying topic.

But the passage continued with "losing control of its nuclear weapons." Only then did it become clear that the danger wasn't post-Communist Russia in its entirety, but a much more specific problem. Make it possessive — "Russia's losing" — and we zip straight through to the danger being researched, which starts with "losing." The reader doesn't need to stop at "Russia" and then shift gears.

This passage in an obituary, however, seemed to be the work of the patella reflex:

> But their son, Christopher, recalled the family's summer sailing expeditions…with Mr. Kennan's navigating through the night on open sea just by dead reckoning.

Was that happy recollection really the navigating, as the apostrophe in "Kennan's" makes it, or was it Mr. Kennan at the helm? The latter seems a lot more likely.

And then there's overkill. Scott J. Burnham, a professor of law at the University of Montana, e-mailed to report an example.

He was sufficiently puzzled by the apostrophe in a reference to the "conceit of adult actors' playing kids," he said, that he wrote to the publication. An editor explained that the apostrophe was needed to avoid a fused participle. But the apparent meaning of the passage — that it is a conceit, an artistic affectation, to cast adult actors as children — was pretty hard to uncover; some inference about conceited actors was almost inevitable. That tiny stroke of ink was being asked to work much too hard.

"I rather like Strunk & White's advice," Mr. Burnham wrote, referring to the esteemed *Elements of Style* by William Strunk Jr. and E. B. White. (It never uses the term "fused participle" but discusses the topic crisply under other headings.) Mr. Burnham's citation: "Any sentence in which the use of the possessive is awkward or impossible should of course be recast."

Absolutely. For example, a recasting that gives us "the conceit of making adult actors portray kids."

Finally, there are times when the difference in meaning between the naked noun or pronoun and the one wearing an apostrophe is microscopic, and ambiguity, if any arises, lasts about a nanosecond. Then the choice really depends on sound. What to do with "I can't imagine him wanting anything less"? This editor left it alone.

# Gantlet/Gauntlet; Stanch/Staunch

### *It All Depends on 'U'*

"Stanch" is a verb meaning to block the flow of something — anything from blood, to a company's financial losses, to emigration. It's also possible to stanch the thing causing the flow — a wound, for example.

"Staunch" — note the "u" — is an adjective meaning watertight (a staunch ship) or more broadly, strong, loyal, dedicated, steadfast (it's popular as a neutral substitute for "zealous").

The words have the same root, and a discernible kinship, and the spelling question used to be considered a toss-up. But the modern consensus is that the twain should not meet, as they did here:

> Finally, Congress has already allocated $1.3 billion to staunch the flow of drugs…

Adding that "u" to the verb is the standard error. Make it "stanch."

A "gantlet" (no "u") is an ordeal, originally military punishment requiring the offender to run between two lines of fellow warriors who beat him with switches, clubs, or other handy toys.

"Gauntlet" (with a "u" and a different root) is a large glove, originally one that protected a combatant's hand and forearm. Throwing down a gauntlet issued a challenge; taking one up accepted the challenge, and both phrases are still used figuratively. So, consider:

> Congress had in fact already erected by statute an intimidating gauntlet of studies, findings, public hearings, and other steps the DOD would need to take before closing a base.

Congress erected an intimidating glove? Drop the "u"; that's a "gantlet."

British journalists and their worldwide followers tend to use only the "u" spellings —"gauntlet" and "staunch" — for all four meanings of the two words. The applicable British ordinance sensibly prescribes different spellings for "stanch" and "staunch," yet no one seems to pay attention. As for the two "g" words, despite their distinctly different origins and meanings (but in line with historical interchangeability in the spellings) only the spelling "gauntlet" seems to be recommended British usage.

The all-purpose "gauntlet" is clearly gaining in this country as well, a couple of Language Corner correspondents pointed out. But some important arbiters still insist on the spelling distinction between a glove and an ordeal. That reasoning triumphs here, as well.

# Gerrymander/Jerry-Built/Jury-Rigged

### *Gerry and His Friends*

Wendy Bryan, the onetime *Columbia Journalism Review* Web captain who took her journalism and Internet skills to the West Coast, e-mailed to ask about "jury-rigged," "jerry-built," and "gerrymander," noting that "I have seen every variation (from jerry-rigged to jury-built), and it seems we all have a hard time keeping it straight."

Gerrymander, the most enjoyable of the three, means to carve up political terrain in outlandish ways for partisan advantage. It celebrates Elbridge Gerry — signer of the Declaration of Independence, governor of Massachusetts, vice president under James Madison — and "salamander." The word was coined to describe a wriggly Massachusetts election district devised when Gerry was governor.

Jerry-built means shoddily put together. Its origin is obscure, but it may be a relative of...

...jury-rigged, a nautical term often appropriated for figurative use ashore, meaning contrived for emergency use, or makeshift. Its origin is also obscure.

"Salamander" is a natural mnemonic for "gerrymander." For the other two, a more pedestrian suggestion: Remember that "jerry" and "build" go together because alphabetically the two come before "jury" and "rig."

# Gibe/Jibe

## *Reverse English?*

The news story said a woman was subjected to "countless jokes and gibes," and that was the right way to use "gibe."

A "gibe" is a taunt, a jeer, a derisive remark, or a teasing joke. As a verb, which is less common, it means to indulge in those things.

So "gibe" was the wrong word when a bureaucracy was described as knowing "only if the card number and the name on the card gibe with its records."

That sentence wanted "jibe," meaning to conform or be in accord, as in "the sets of numbers do jibe." (Aboard ship, "jibe" means to shift a sail from one side to the other.)

Some references declare the two spellings interchangeable for the two very different words, and that isn't helpful at all.

Then how to remember which is which? Well ... the one that means "jeer" or "joke" does NOT start with a "j."

# Gild/Paint the Lily

### *Brush Up Your Shakespeare, Act I*

The original phrase whence cometh this common error is usable just the way himself wrote it:

> If you want to *gild the lily*, you could add herbs or minced garlic to the cheese layer [emphasis added; the phrase in italics is the problem].

In *King John*, some of the nobles are discussing his majesty's plans to have himself crowned a second time. To do so, says one, would be "wasteful and ridiculous excess," as it would be "To gild refined gold, to paint the lily..."

So our example is off on two counts: It seems to mean adding a finishing touch or a flourish, but Shakespeare meant going overboard. And it abuses the original, lovely phrasing. Let's face it, the guy had an ear. And an eye.

Now comes a television quiz program whose three contestants were asked to come up with an expression dealing with excess and — the two critical words — "derived from" Shakespeare. All answered "gild the lily," and all were correct, given the sneaky wording. And an opportunity to do a bit of educating went by the boards.

Anyone is free to say "gild the lily," of course; it's one of the world's most popular misquotations. For that matter, anyone can say "fricassee the lily." What no one should do is suggest that Shakespeare wrote anything of the sort except "paint the lily."

*Other matters Shakespearean appear in Honored in the Breach; Wherefore; and Raveled Sleave, with an "A."*

# (I Am) Good/(I Am) Well
## *Well and Good, It Would Seem*

Laura Manes, then a summer intern at the *National Post* in Canada, e-mailed with an interesting question about "the jarring 'I am good' that seems to have become the universal response to 'How are you?'" Ms. Manes thought she might be "the only twenty-something person I know that still replies, 'I am well, thank you.'"

Uneasiness about "good" in such an exchange involves its potential for ambiguity — are we talking about virtue here, or talent, or just state of mind? But "well," so often used to describe health, can be ambiguous, too.

As a practical matter, either word works. Both function as adjectives following "am," so the adverbial sense of "well" isn't in play. And context — or in speech, inflection — is very likely to make clear what "good" or "well" means, even in the rare instance when "I am (feel) good" is intended as a boast about morality.

# 'Graduated College'
## *But not with Honors*

"Hey, ejenk," Charlie McDonald e-mailed from Las Cruces, N.M., where he is retired as a high school English teacher but active as a freelance writer and weekend singer-guitarist, "how about jumping on 'He graduated Harvard in 1966'"?

Clearly appalled at having heard a famous broadcaster say that, Mr. McDonald added, "Zounds!"

Zounds it is. "Graduated Harvard" (or anyplace else) is a common error; the phrase needs "from." Technically, it's the institution that does the graduating — moving the student up a grade — and some traditionalists still hold out for "was graduated from." The "was" is uncommon these days, but the "from" is not optional if we don't want to look illiterate.

# Graffito/Graffiti

### *It Takes Two...*

O r more. This was fun, but it wasn't quite right:

Graffiti is illegal — but it's a beautiful crime.

When only one piece of amateur artwork adorns an otherwise bare wall, there's a nice, useful word for it: "graffito." The word in our example — used as a singular, as it so commonly is — is the plural.

After that paragraph appeared on the Web, some challenging e-mail came from Dennis Moran, assistant business editor of the *Prague Post*. "English borrows copiously if incompletely," he wrote, noting such Associated Press style preferences as "referendums" and "stadiums" (not the Latin plurals "referenda" and "stadia"). (Amen to those, and to "curriculums," rather than the pompous "curricula" still widely favored in academic circles. And anyone using "fora" instead of "forums" should never be let loose off campus.)

Mr. Moran went on:

In the court of common usage, it seems to me that "graffiti" won out long ago as both singular and plural. Actually, it seems to me that in English it's an uncountable noun, like "grass." The word refers to the phenomenon, and doesn't count scrawlings.

Outside of archeological and other scholarly writing, where the singular has uniformly been distinguished from the plural, the word is a relatively recent arrival in English, dating only from the 1960s. And though the plural (with or without a plural verb) is more common — as are the multiple scrawlings it defines — the singular, when appropriate, still has defenders among writers and experts on usage. It's a nicety worth preserving. It's also a sweet kind of word, as Mr. Moran suggested in a subsequent note:

> Actually, I'd love it if people used the word "graffito," I guess because I love Italian words...But I never hear it, so it seems to me doomed.

It isn't if writers and editors decide it isn't; we can still use it when one bit of writing is all we're talking about. It would be a shame if we could no longer say, should the occasion arise, "A lone grafitto graced the chapel wall."

# Hand Down/Hand Up

## *The Only Way to Go Is...*

A headline reported, "Grand Jury Hands Down Murder Indictment," and that was a misdirection.

By widely accepted custom, indictments and verdicts are handed up by juries to a higher judicial authority, a judge. The transmission can also be described with "return" or "deliver" or "issue."

It's judges who hand things down: rulings, decisions, verdicts in nonjury trials, and so on.

# Hanged/Hung

## *Pictures and People*

A visitor to the Language Corner Web site wondered about this passage from a magazine article about an archeological discovery:

> The majority of the people had not died from natural causes. Most had been hung — the ropes were around their necks — hit over the head or stabbed.

As a past tense for the word meaning to put to death by hanging, "hung" is accepted by some dictionaries as one alternative. Most modern authorities, though, still argue that pictures are hung and people are hanged. That distinction is useful only because those authorities say it is.

# Have To/Got To

## *Poetry and Prose*

The headline "You've Got to Be Carefully Taught" (See *Police, the*), which first appeared in the *Columbia Journalism Review*, alluded to a wonderful song of that title from *South Pacific* about the unnaturalness of bigotry. It prompted a mild complaint from Michele Drier, a longtime California newspaper reporter and editor.

She enjoyed the allusion, she said, but was concerned

> ...that "you've got" is creeping into the language as the correct form — thanks to AOL, "You've Got Mail" became the title of the remake of "Shop Around the Corner." I have even caught myself saying "what have you got" to people other than my dog.

So for the record, and with thanks for the reminder, "have to" is the preferable phrasing for such things unless we're clearly striving for the colloquial — was AOL? — or maybe writing a song.

# Head/Head Up

## *Wrong Heading*

Two detectives, the novelist wrote, "were called in to head up the investigation." That was excessive by two letters: "u" and "p."

The expression "head up" is common, and pretty far down on the list of usage sins. But the "up" contributes nothing to sense and to many people looks semiliterate.

"Head" does the job — so do "run" or "direct" or "supervise" or lots of other alternatives.

# Heart-Rending/Heart-Wrenching

## *A Wrenching Tale*

Louis Trager, an editor in the San Francisco Bay area, e-mailed with an unhappy observation about idioms and their mutations:

> The one I see and hear regularly now that I'm attuned to it is "heart-wrenching," a mismatch of "heart-rending" and "gut-wrenching."

"Rend" means to tear. "Heart-rending" means distressing, causing emotional pain, arousing deep sympathy. It can be used to describe either an experience or an account of one:

> Prosecutors had summoned almost four dozen victims and relatives who gave heart-rending testimony that left some jurors discreetly wiping their eyes.

"Wrench" means to twist violently. And in a nice economy, "wrenching" all by itself is synonymous with "heart-rending." That makes "heart-wrenching" redundant even though it's structurally defensible. And the apparent mismatching sounds ignorant.

With "heart-rending" and "wrenching" and lots of other choices available we don't really need "heart-wrenching," and at the time of this writing the coinage has largely been ignored by dictionaries.

But it may well be the wave of the future. As Mr. Trager noted with regret, electronic evidence puts "heart-wrenching" ahead by roughly two to one.

# He or She, etc.

## *He, She, and Changing Times*

Dale Brayden, a software engineer in Vancouver, Wash., sent a thoughtful e-mail after reading the entry Singular Noun, Plural Pronoun (which see). The entry criticizes the common but deplorable use of plural pronouns for singular nouns, in this case "they" for "bond firm." The solution was obvious — use "it," not "they" — but that ducked a tougher question. Mr. Brayden recalled,

> Years ago, I would have written, for example, "no person should feel any pressure simply because he was called by the City Budget Director."

But "he," the default pronoun for generations of us, is inarguably sexist. Granting that, Mr. Brayden had no sympathy for the faddish coinage "s/he," which happily has not seemed to catch on. And simply alternating "she" with "he," willy-nilly and regardless of context, can be conspicuous and distracting. The gender-neutral "one," as in "One should not feel...because one was called..." has "a tendency to proliferate," Mr. Brayden observed, and "sounds awfully upper-crusty and stilted." It certainly does.

What to do? Despite some evidence in well-edited publications of a spreading acceptance for "they" in such cases — especially after "anyone," "everyone," and the like — we don't seem to be there yet. The instances are rare enough that they may be nothing more than momentary lapses into the habits of speech, as opposed to those of writing.

In contexts that are clearly male or clearly female — and excepting many generic references to occupations — the pronoun of the appropriate gender is, uh, appropriate, and we needn't strain to avoid it.

Elsewhere, a broad answer is to rework the sentence; a narrow example of reworking is to use plurals: "People should not feel pressure...because they were called..."

Mr. Brayden said he saw "he or she" often and found it "awkward and inelegant," but for now it's a legitimate last resort. Maybe, if we can avoid drumbeat repetition, it will come to seem as comfortable as "he."

This passage, reporting on a poll, avoided the "he or she" problem at a price:

> ...Mr. Giuliani and Mrs. Clinton (neither has officially announced candidacy) are in a statistical dead heat.

The absence of any pronoun before "candidacy" was noticeably awkward. Maybe "a candidacy" would have seemed more natural. Or duck the issue with "neither has officially decided to run."

Or maybe even "neither has officially announced his or her candidacy." Unlike the generic "he or she" situations that crop up so frequently, this was a case of a real he and a real she.

*See also Collective Nouns; and Tons Was.*

# Historic/Historical

See Adviser/Advisor

# Hitting Milestones

## *Watch Out for the Rocks!*

Alex McKale, a research and development manager at Hewlett-Packard, heard the phrase "hit a milestone" and thought it odd. "Wouldn't hitting a milestone damage the vehicle," he asked by e-mail, "and thereby hinder further progress?"

Well, yes. A metaphor should work literally as well as figuratively, and hitting real stones isn't a positive experience.

Holding that thought, we'd expect to find the athlete in this headline being worked on in the trainer's room, or the emergency room: "Veteran Defenseman Bodger Hits Milestone." And this poor little guy had a real run of bad luck: "Calvin, 11 months old, has been hitting developmental milestones."

A quick Nexis search found some variation of "hit a milestone" used over 1,000 times in less than a year. That may not be worth losing sleep over, but why risk the risible? We're better off letting people and things reach milestones or pass milestones, not run into them.

# Hold (Down) the Fort

## *Fly Away Home?*

People often seem to engage in a strange task:

...someone to hold down the fort...

She would simply hold down the fort...

His wife holds down the fort...

The expression those passages missed is "hold the fort." It may have originated on the early American frontier, or in a nineteenth-century American hymn, and it means hold on till I get there, or take care of things while I'm away, or don't give an inch, or hang in there.

Regardless, there's no "down" in it.

Mark W. Freeman (see Wangle/Wrangle) seethes when he reads about forts being held down. In an e-mail suggesting an edict on the topic, he noted with typical justifiable indignation, "A fort is not a hot air balloon."

Ah, but wait. Comes the show-business bible *Daily Variety* with an article about heightened interest, after the devastation caused by Hurricane Katrina in 2005, in retrofitting California buildings to keep them in place in natural disasters (notably earthquakes).

And what's the headline? What else?

Hold Down the Fort

# Home/Hone

## *It's Not a Hone Run, Either*

M ark W. Freeman, this time to depose as follows:

I deplore the use of "hone" for "home," as in "the critic was honing in on his target." What I deplore even more is the tendency of dictionaries to accept usages such as this on the ground that "lots of people make this mistake." Lots of people say "chimbly" for "chimney," but because they aren't TV news anchors, the dictionaries haven't accepted this. Yet.

And not soon, one hopes. "Home in on," meaning aim at, narrow a field to, apparently evolved from the homing performed by pigeons, and then by airplanes and missiles as they headed for targets. It's certainly more logical than a phrase that evokes a razor strop.

# Honored in the Breach

## *Brush Up Your Shakespeare, Act II*

Here, as often happens with this allusion, the great man's meaning is turned around:

> Perhaps it is a saving grace of Russian politics these days that laws and orders are honored more in the breach than in the observance.

What the modern writer meant was that the laws and orders were broken more often than they were obeyed. But Hamlet, who said it first, meant something else.

When he described his stepfather's boozy carryings-on as a custom "more honored in the breach than the observance," he meant that it was a bad custom, more honored when violated than when followed. Not the same thing, and the pretty phrase is usable in its original sense.

*Other matters Shakespearean appear in Gild/Paint the Lily; Wherefore; and Raveled Sleave, with an "A."*

# Hopefully

A perfectly reasonable way to start a sentence unless there's a real, not imaginary, danger of ambiguity. See Important/Importantly.

# Human Race

See Oddities

# Hyphens

------------------------------------------------------------

## *Those Wild and Crazy Hyphens*

Stacy Moore, managing editor of the *Hi-Desert Star* in Yucca Valley, Calif., e-mailed to ask about hyphenation, a topic that could fill a book (now there's a chilling thought). She and a writer at the paper differed over whether to hyphenate "big city," "beach front," and "ice cold" as compound adjectives in front of nouns. Ms. Moore concluded, "I say hyphenate 'em all."

Agreed.

The classic reason for using hyphens with compounds is to avoid ambiguity. The hyphen links two or more words instantly for the reader's rapidly moving eye. "Big-city" is a perfect example. A "big city man" is a large man from a city. A "big-city man" is a man from a large city, and the hyphen is mandatory to pull the two words together to make one modifier. "Forty-odd employees" would be silly without the hyphen. So would "small-business man" (which requires splitting "businessman" in two).

Beyond that, "big-city" just wants a hyphen because convention calls for it. And, even though they're not likely to be misunderstood when they're hyphen-free, that's also true of "beach-front" (also reasonable as one word, noun and adjective) and "ice-cold."

Or so it says here. Some decisions about hyphens, especially decisions about what convention requires, are open to argument. And because of largely arbitrary choices involving style, the same compounds will appear hyphenated in one good publication and unadorned in another.

Furthermore...

In the third paragraph in this entry, the phrase "rapidly moving" combines an adverb and a (verbal) adjective to form one modifier describing "eye." Yet the compound takes no hyphen. That's because the adverbial ending "ly" is almost universally considered to perform the bridging function that a hyphen would otherwise take care of.

"Very" also needs no hyphen to link it to an adjective, by common consent — "very popular singer." It's just an adverb modifying an adjective. So, usually, are "most," "more," "least," "less," and other such words used in phrases like "most beloved teacher," "least likely outcome," and "less complex solution."

That last was published with a hyphen, and there's no reason for one. Nor was there in "the nation's most-populous state" or "several more-famous plays," also hyphenated in print. An exception with "most" is the Federal Bureau of Investigation's Most-Wanted List. It's not a list that is somehow most wanted, it's "most" and "wanted" linked to make one adjective describing "list." It needs a clarifying hyphen.

(John Kilkenny of Melbourne, Australia, waded through this "lucubration" [as he called it, not kindly but justifiably] on the Web and begged to differ with one example. The phrase "several more-famous plays," he e-mailed, needs a hyphen to say that the plays are more famous than the one being discussed. With no hyphen, it can be read to mean — our bugaboo ambiguity rearing its head — several additional plays that, like this one, were famous. The hyphen seems unusually unattractive in such a phrase, but without rewording, it's defensible unless the context is totally clear.)

In deciding whether to use a hyphen, it may be useful — and, of course, it may be maddening — to remember that printed lines can break in funny places. Look how these broke:

...he was the longest

...along came a figure

...said one of the deportees...a heavy

...many officials recall how Mr. Bush's father seemed ill

This is how those passages continued:

> serving of the chief rabbis in Europe
>
> skating scandal at the Winter Games
>
> equipment operator
>
> attuned to economic conditions

The guidelines for clarity or convention or both seem to require hyphens after all of those end-of-line words; their placement just compounds the problem when the hyphens are omitted. (The same guidelines surely called for a hyphen in the phrase "infectious disease expert," which was a tad risible without one, and "obstruction of justice laws," which was just a tad tough to read.)

The subject is far from exhausted, but the writer isn't. A closing thought from John Benbow, once editor of the stylebook of the Oxford University Press, quoted in the *Harper Dictionary of Contemporary Usage,* by William Morris and Mary Morris: "If you take hyphens seriously, you will surely go mad."

Are we there yet?

# 'If Not'

## *Fatally Fuzzy*

In the passages below, and in thousands like them, the little phrase "if not" is inescapably sloppy; it can also be seriously unfair.

> ...at worst, he bullied his opponents and impugned their integrity, if not their patriotism.
>
> Off and on for two decades, Dr. Lee's behavior was curious, if not criminal.

"If not" in both cases achieves the rarefied status of perfect ambiguity.

Did the writer mean that the subject in the first passage actually stopped short of attacking his opponents' patriotism? Did the second writer mean Dr. Lee's behavior was probably not criminal? Distinct possibilities, but the terse yet flabby "if not" doesn't get the reader there.

Or, perhaps more likely in these examples (and more commonly), "if not" could mean the writers wanted to imply guilt without quite coming out with the charge. That's dirty pool. Whatever meaning is intended, saying it directly — and providing supporting evidence later — is the responsible way to go.

A third distinct possibility, a cousin of the second, is that a writer doesn't have a clue but wants to slip in the possibility of something ugly, just in case. Again, unfair.

Judging from the context in each case, the writer of the first passage would have been more candid had he written "and at times even their patriotism"; the writer of the second seemed to mean "…curious, and quite possibly criminal." But those are guesses, the only recourse left to us by "if not."

Guesswork came up with a different reading when an article reported that a procedural step "will delay, if not scuttle, an investigation…" That writer, the rest of the article suggested, meant "…delay, though not necessarily scuttle…"

At least, that may have been it. Who knows?

# Impact, the Verb

## *Hard-Hitting?*

When asked to tell a story that impacted her character…

…U.S. Gulf Coast operations were significantly impacted…

…notices to each individual impacted by the law…

…warmer weather…impacted electricity use…

The drumbeat has a purpose: to bring home the reality that "impact," as a synonym for the verb "affect," will not go away. Sad but almost certainly true.

"Impact," the noun, denotes the striking of one object by another or the force of such a collision. The word was also used as a verb for centuries, but until the last one it just meant to pack or pack in, as with a really angry tooth.

Then, sometime in mid-century, apparently, somebody thought "impact" sounded like a power verb, and a stunning number of people went along.

"Impact" in the sense that offends many of us is everywhere. Even the few publications that make a point of avoiding it end up quoting it frequently because so many other people use it.

Except for such quoting, nothing requires any of us to use "impact" as a verb (except for teeth, or for heavenly bodies colliding). And maybe we grumps are overreacting. In any case, stamping it out would require moving mountains.

# Implement

See Reader's Potpourri

# Imply/Infer

## *Think 'M' before 'N'*

To imply is to suggest, hint, get an idea across — deliberately or by accident — without saying or writing it in so many words. Politician A might not quite say politician B was a crook, but he certainly might want to make his audience think so, in which case he would imply. Implying is an act.

It would be up to the audience to infer. That means to read or listen to something and deduce, or guess, what is meant. Inferring is a thought process.

The confusion between the words is a lot more common than it should be and almost always involves "infer":

- A government official issued an apology for "inferring that a fourteen-year-old girl might have instigated a sexual relationship with a clergyman." What he inferred didn't matter; what he got in trouble for was putting the thought into words — implying it.
- A writer discoursing on a denizen of the deep — the horseshoe leatherjacket, no less — declared, "As the name infers, this fish has a horseshoe-shaped pattern on the side of its tough thick skin." A name can't infer, but it can imply.

A stab at mnemonics: First someone may iMply, then someone else may iNfer — "m" before "n." Or the sPeaker imPlies. Or one INfers, as in INgests, as in takes IN...Or maybe...

# Important/Importantly

## *Important? Well, Interesting*

Steve Parrott, then associate director (later director) for university relations at the University of Iowa, e-mailed to ask, "Please consider a few words on "more important/more importantly."

Okay. Mr. Parrott had in mind sentences or clauses that begin with one of those phrases, like

> Most importantly, the charges are tied directly to the original topic Mr. Starr was supposed to investigate.

The short answer is that either form of the word is acceptable. *Merriam-Webster's Dictionary of English Usage* has a lengthy and interesting (really) discussion of the longstanding argument (really) over important versus importantly, with many citations, and concludes that "both are defensible grammatically and both are in respectable use."

The tilt here, though, is toward "importantly," the adverb in the case. The critical point in its favor is that it can stand alone at the start of a sentence or clause, without "more" or "most" or any other modifier. "Important," the adjective, can't.

Try it. Drop "most" from the example quoted; the sentence still works. Then, with "most" gone, drop the "ly" from "importantly"; the sentence no longer works.

A mindless aversion to "ly" adverbs for openers — an extension of misguided rigidity about "importantly"? — must have been at work in the following passage, since no human being ever spoke this way: "Not surprising, a variety of polls indicate…" Try dropping "not" from *that.*

And the arguments for "most important" (along with its spawn) are strained, as an e-mail conversation with the freelance copy editor Christy Goldfinch of Fort Worth made clear.

Since "important" commonly fails to clearly modify any specific part of its sentence, the adjective advocates contend that it can be understood to modify the whole thing — a "sentence adjective." Well, "importantly" can certainly be called a "sentence adverb."

But with "importantly" there's no need for that dance; save it for emergencies. The adverb has an element to grab hold of within its sentence: the verb or the overall predicate.

In fact, that reality refutes the literalists' arguments against "hopefully" or any other adverb at the start of a sentence. (Nothing in this sermon should be construed as enthusiasm for "Firstly," an irritating start for an even more irritating series.)

Another argument for "Most important" is that the phrase "What is" is understood to precede it. If that were a natural supposition, all sorts of adjectives (with modifiers) could start sentences. But "Most happy, the storm ended" just doesn't make it.

"Most important" is acceptable — not preferable — not on logical grounds but because it is widely used and well established; idiom wins that limited argument. And in passages that start with modifiers ending in "ly" — "equally" comes to mind — using "important" is handy. By and large, though, "most importantly" is by far the better choice.

## Incidence/Incident/Instance

### *'In' Words*

It seemed to John Fisher Smith of Ashland, Ore., a writer of aural essays for radio, that he was encountering evidence of confusion over three similar-sounding words among reporters and even "folks in cabinet positions who ought to know better."

In alphabetical order, the words are "incidence," "incident," and "instance."

"Incidence" is the only one of the three that is not a synonym for "event." It means the frequency or rate at which something happens:

> Officials have seen the incidence of child abuse drop off.
>
> The incidence of U.S. children and teens with a disabling condition...

"Incident" means occurrence, event. It is often used in a negative context and in fact can be a synonym for trouble or difficulty, as in "the arrest was made without incident." (Things obviously happen *with* incident, but nobody ever says that.)

"A series of firebombing incidents" was acceptable, though "incident" strikes many people as too trivial-sounding for true calamity or major crime. It would be painfully strange to describe as "incidents" the attacks of 9/11/01 or the great hurricanes of 2005.

"Instance" is the most versatile of the three words. It also means an occurrence, but commonly one that represents or is part of a larger pattern. A synonym is "example" — consider "for instance."

By extension, the word can mean "case" or "situation":

No instances of identity theft have been reported.

In numerous instances...she declined to provide dates.

In certain instances, we do close down bridges.

But how to remember which spelling we want? The only answer seems to be regular consultation with Professor Rote.

# Individuals/People/Persons

### *People Need People*

The article attributed new developments in a banking scandal to "individuals who have direct knowledge of the investigation."

Why "individuals"? Why not "people"? The answer is that bureaucratese is infectious.

At times it's necessary to distinguish between individuals and groups, so "individual," singular and plural, has its uses as a noun. Otherwise, such solid old English words as "man," "woman," and "people" are just fine. And "people" is almost always preferable to the stilted "persons," except on signs about restaurant occupancy, where the bureaucrats rule.

After reading that paragraph in the *Columbia Journalism Review*, Margo Young, director of academic publications at the University of Nebraska–Lincoln College of Business Administration, e-mailed with a question.

She noted that in *Elements of Style* by Strunk and White, a guide for generations of American expository writers, "persons" gets preference for some contexts. The good book declares:

> The word people is best not used with words of number, in place of persons. If of "six people" five went away, how many people would be left behind? Answer: one people.

Citing that passage, Ms. Young asked, "Whom should we use today as the standard: Streisand or Strunk and White?"

As respected as Strunk and White are and should be, we're better off with Streisand on this one. "Persons" has never seemed natural, but a lot of us learned to use it years ago as part of the near-ubiquitous Associated Press style. Times change. It's no longer style at the AP or, also in a change, at the *New York Times*. Both prescribe "people" except for such established idioms as "displaced persons" and "missing persons."

And the Strunk and White argument didn't really make sense. If we started with 45,000 people (would anyone, anywhere, say "persons"?) at a football game, and all but one left the stadium, how many, and what, would be left? Answer: one person. That's what would be left in the Strunk and White example, too. For centuries, the natural, standard English plural for "person" has been "people." And S & W to the contrary notwithstanding, using "people" as an all-purpose plural never locked anyone into using "people" as a singular.

## 'In History'

See 'Ever'; 'In History'

## In Line/On Line, Online

See In, Up, and On

# In Order to

## *To Be Brief...*

An e-mail questioner wondered why people kept saying "in order to" when "to" was all they needed, and it's a fair question. None of these needed the extra words:

> In order to demonstrate this struggle...
>
> Incorporate the business in order to take advantage...
>
> ...what others need to do in order to get there.

But what about this one?

> ...to preserve our present in order to build a better future.

At a minimum, that would be unpleasing — choppy, unrhythmic — without "in order," and it might even be confusing.

"In order" can usually be omitted, or deleted in editing, but any hard-and-fast rule is dangerous. Once in a while the phrase is needed to avoid (not, in this case, "in order to avoid") misunderstanding.

# In, Up, and On

## *Three Very Little Words*

Linda Leonhardt, a decorative painter in Great River, N.Y., e-mailed to report a domestic dispute:

> My husband and I were hotly discussing "between and in between" the other day, and we haven't settled a thing.

"In" is clearly unnecessary in a phrase like "in between the pages" and in most standard writing is probably best omitted. Yet the "in" doesn't do any real harm and may just add a sense of precision or specificity lacking in an unaccompanied "between" (just as "in there, up there," and so on can be more informative than a mere "there"). And unlike the single word "between," "in between" sounds natural standing on its own: the fighters charged each other, and the referee was caught in between.

When a writer said "I called up" a source, Phil Dechman, a retired editor at the *Independent* in Grimsby, Ontario, was reminded of a conversation at a gathering of his parents and some of their friends when he was a child. He recalled in an e-mail that "the use of 'up' was denigrated, after which one sharpie raised his glass and offered the toast, 'Bottoms!'" But in "call up," Mr. Dechman suggested, the "up" is always redundant. And so it is, unless we're talking about military forces. "Call up" may fit in intentionally casual or conversational writing, though.

As Wendy Bryan, then a Web specialist at the Columbia Journalism School, noted, "online" (one word) has become an all-purpose word for the Internet universe. But she was puzzled when she read about someone who "stood on line at the bank machine," and wondered, "Do I get behind those on line, or may I remain in line?"

"On line" is apparently a regionalism; the *New York Times Manual of Style and Usage* declares, "Few besides New Yorkers speak of standing on line. Follow the usage of the rest of the English-speaking world: in line." The "on" version may be spreading, but "in" is still the unassailable choice.

# Interface

See Reader's Potpourri

# Invoke

See Evoke/Invoke

# Irrelevant (NOT 'Irrevelant')

### *Relevant, as in Middle East*

There's an old name for the lands just east of the Mediterranean — "Levant" — that can help us avoid some trouble with a couple of much more commonly used words.

One article applauded a "very strong, revelant message to the people." Another deplored the "devilishly clever labels on a collection of random, irrevelant scenes."

Typos both, maybe, and an easy slip to make. But a database search suggests that a widespread switching of middle syllables — "v-e-l" replacing "l-e-v" — is going on out there. That strong message was "relevant." Those scenes were "irrelevant."

To avoid the misspellings, it may help to think of "relate," sort of a cousin of "relevant." But that will carry us only as far as the "l" in the correct spellings (a critical place to reach, though). So "levant," with the appropriate prefix, may be the best mnemonic. And there are extra showoff points for working "Levant" into conversation.

# 'Issues'

### *Got a Problem? Say So!*

Through his pain, Robert Brown found a bit of humor:

> One day will you please address the "issue/problem" issue (er, problem). In my dictionary, I don't see "problem" as a definition for "issue." Everyone is using "issue" in a problematic way (when will there be "issuematic?").

This collection has generally omitted discussion of fads precisely because of their impermanence. But the note from Mr. Brown — who lives in New York City, owns an art gallery, and writes about gastronomy on the side, he said in response to a query — touched a nerve. The "issue" fad has been as sweeping as any in memory. The word is used in countless sloppy ways. And unlike such pomposity as "at this point in time," "issue" is effortless and threatens to become a plague.

A weatherman warns of "cloudiness issues." A sports announcer notes a team's "penalty issues." And from the print world:

- "health issues, such as high blood sugar"
- the college whose chief, according to a news article, "wants the mold issue resolved"
- radio stations that "bombarded their listeners with the issue"

As a standard-English alternative to the wimpy "issue," we should certainly consider the straightforward "problem" — or "concern" or "weakness" or "question" or "topic" or "matter" or...

# Jerry-Built; Jury-Rigged

See Gerrymander

# Jibe

See Gibe

# Late, as in Dead

### *Grave Concerns*

"The late Joe Jones" is a concise, handy way of pointing out that Joe is dead. But literal-minded critics object to "the late" in many contexts because if read with determination to be literal, it can seem to mean somebody did something after the last sunset.

"The late Joe Jones wrote three novels" would fail the test with such critics, but in fact no reasonable person could misread it, and the alternatives can be tortured or silly or both.

"At the time of his death Joe Jones had written three novels" avoids any suspicion of ghostly activity, but it's a needlessly long way home. "Joe Jones wrote three novels before his death" is at least a little redundant, since he could hardly have written them afterward (which is *not* to suggest that "before his death" and "before he died" and the like may never be used, in their place).

One usage book suggests that "the late" means not just "the dead" but "the now dead." That's an interesting notion, but expecting readers to be aware of it, even subconsciously, seems overly optimistic.

We can go ahead and use "the late" most of the time and just ignore the moans of the literalists. We do need to be alert to situations where it can be genuinely ambiguous, or where it's bound to be funny, but alert is the name of the game, no?

# Lend/Loan

## *Very Well, a Loan*

"If he could spare the money," the popular novelist wrote, "he'd gladly loan it to me." Why take a perfectly good noun and make it a verb when there's already a perfectly good verb?

A loan is what you get when somebody lends you something. Afterward, you say he lent you something. Or has lent or had lent or will have lent.

# Lie, Lay, and All That

## *Lie This to Rest?*

No, of course not. But the confusion between "lie" and "lay" was different and subtler in a passage that said someone who maneuvered for a job too overtly "did not do what a shrewd operator would do and lay low."

Someone was thinking of "to lie low," meaning to hunker down, make oneself inconspicuous. Introduced by "did not," as it was in the example, the verb required the present tense: the job candidate "did not...lie low."

"To lie" means to rest, be at rest, repose, or just exist on or in some place (the fault lies with the captain, not the crew) or in some condition or position (lie low, lie down). "Lay" is the past tense of "lie" — he lay low for awhile. The participle is "lain" — until that day, she had lain low.

That is to say, lie, lay, lain.

Probably because that past tense is "lay," that word is often confused with...

..."to lay," meaning to put or place something somewhere (including to bring forth an egg). This one takes an object — lay that pistol down, babe — and no form of "to lie" does. (Well, "lie your heart out," but that's another "lie.") The past tense of "lay" is "laid," and so is its participle.

Thus, the hit trio lay, laid, laid.

The murder suspect, the article reported, "laid low, escaping suspicion..." But he didn't put something (except himself) someplace, so he "lay low." Lie, lay, lain. (If someone had killed him in a barroom brawl, we might say he'd been "laid low," and that it was time to "lay him to rest." After his funeral, he'd have been "laid in his grave." Lay, laid, laid.)

Another article said, "Priests muttered the final prayers as the bodies were lain on pyres of sandalwood." But "lain" is the participle of "lie" and nothing else but that, and it can't be used that way. The right word was "laid," meaning placed, put, deposited. Lay, laid, laid.

The failure to distinguish between "lie" and "lay" is widely considered illiterate, yet it's surprisingly common. Is the only answer rote memorization? Seems so, but anyone with a mnemonic trick that has helped avoid the confusion is welcome to send it along.

# 'Lightening'; 'Forecasted'

## *Lightening Was Forecasted?*

Lisa Aug of the Office of Communications at the Kentucky Cabinet for Families and Children found this on a television network's Web site:

> Powerful storms are forecasted for parts of the region again tonight.

"Forecasted?" Ms. Aug asked, in obvious dismay.

Alas, some major dictionaries do give that form as a second-choice past tense, and it turns up a lot. But it looks and sounds like an error. "Forecast" does the job for the past as well as the present.

As it does for the verbs "broadcast" and, while we're at it, "cast."

In the same spot, Ms. Aug also found a report, about fires in the West, that was "spelling the electrical phenomenon 'lightening.'" That's also surprisingly common, but fortunately the dictionaries don't seem to support it, even as a copout alternative. The word is "lightning" — no "e" — unless something is becoming, literally or figuratively, less weighty or less dark. Lightning, as it happens, has a lightening effect on the sky.

# Like/Such As

## *Given a Choice, Say Thanks*

The voice of experience: Long arguments erupt on the question of "like" versus "such as." Quickly then: Both are perfectly fine.

The question (not the argument) came up in a note from Martin Schneider, a copy editor of academic titles in the New York area. He recalled from his magazine days a conversation, topic lost to memory, in which someone said, "Right, it's like the 'like' or 'such as' distinction."

So is there really a difference, Mr. Schneider wondered, between "Nobel winners like Einstein and Feynman" and "Nobel winners such as Einstein and Feynman"?

Not a particle. If we took "A player like DiMaggio never quits" and made it say "A player such as DiMaggio never quits" would the meaning — or the sound — be improved? The chorus of "nos" is deafening.

Yet some people would insist that because "like" can mean "similar to" or "resembling," our sentence using "like" would refer to *other* Nobel winners who are somehow *like* Einstein and Feynman, but *not* to the two men themselves, and that with "like" we would *not* be including DiMaggio in our salute to grit.

That is unreasonably literalistic, unrealistically restrictive, and not even logical. Look closely at "such as": It's no more precise than "like."

In any case, "like" and "such as" are used interchangeably by fine writers — and of course are universally understood — every five minutes. Once in a blue moon, "like" can be ambiguous. But if we banished all phrasings that carry that risk, we'd be back to grunts and flailing arms.

No one is forced to use "like." Some people (and some publications, it seems) refuse to do so. Other people (and at least one prominent publication) actually prefer "like," and the preference can lead to a refusal to use "such as." That rigidity is as wrongheaded as the other one.

Closing the e-mail conversation, Mr. Schneider put his philosophy this way:

> I always say that the ideal editor is an "unpedantic pedant."

Well said.

# Like, with a Clause

## *That Ole Devil 'Like'*

No, not the one in "John likes Mary." And not the weird but widespread affliction of such expressions as "It's, like, cool"; that's not worth talking about in a place like this. Our topic is the "like" that compares things. This one, by continuing consensus, was wrong:

> …like Edwards and his Jets did…

"Like" is being used with the meaning "similar to," which obviously wouldn't work in that fragment. (Try it.) The rule of thumb is this: Don't use "like" if what follows is a clause — a noun (including a name) or pronoun that is the subject of its own verb. The phrase "Edwards and his Jets" is the subject of "did," and it clearly won't sit still for "similar to."

So it should be "as Edwards and his Jets did" or — and this often sounds more natural — "the way" they did. In speech, the form "like they did" is virtually universal. For even moderately formal writing, our rule of thumb remains much the safest bet. At least for now.

But confusion abounds with "like." Consider

> the current wave of terror, *as* the ones before it, represents…
> [emphasis added]

Someone — writer or editor — was afraid of "like," probably because there was a verb nearby. But the phrase between commas has no verb of its own; "represents," despite the parenthetical interruption, has "wave of terror" for its subject. "Like the ones before it" was right choice.

In a similar situation, this emerged:

> Some of the better entries will, as Noah Baumbach's "Squid and the Whale" did last year, secure sizable deals...

Fear of "like" because a verb was involved? Or just fondness for the cumbersome? Regardless, a more natural phrasing is

> ...entries, like Noah Baumbach's "Squid and the Whale" last year, will secure...

The parenthetical clause of which "like" is a part has no verb of its own, so our preposition commits neither felony nor misdemeanor. (And the tortured, hold-your-breath-till-I-finish division of the verb "will secure" is irritating, though technically acceptable; see Adverb Placement).

A couple of generations ago, smoking was encouraged with the catchy phrase "Winston tastes good, like a cigarette should." After loud grumbling by schoolteachers and others, that was changed to the simpering "Winston tastes good, as a cigarette should."

Flat? Overly strict? Yes. Maybe so bad it helped people stop smoking.

# Lion's Share

## *Most Is Still a Lot*

In Aesop's fable "The Lion's Share," the lion and three lesser beasts go hunting together and kill a stag, whereupon the lion decides he'll keep it all for himself.

With that background, some purists (a couple of whom e-mailed this cubicle) insist that "the lion's share" can mean only the entire thing, whatever it is.

But the language moves along, sometimes irresistibly. The phrase clearly has evolved over centuries to connote "whatever the lion wants," and thus "the majority" or "most." And that's just fine.

The shift is so pronounced, in fact, that if it seems urgent to make "the lion's share" mean "all," we'd better plan on writing footnotes.

# Literally

### *But It Just Ain't So!*

A couple of e-mail guests have complained about the use of the words "literal" and "literally" as if they meant, literally, "figurative" and "figuratively." One correspondent, having assumed that the Supreme Court building was electrically up to date, was startled to hear that the court was "literally burning the midnight oil."

Well, there are heavier offenses, but why do we need "literally," when it's the opposite of the truth, to make a point? Besides that, it's awfully tired. Surely we can find other ways.

# Loath/Loathe

### *If This Isn't Loath...*

Pick a winner: The villain in the novel said, "That I am *loath* to do." The newspaper article said, "It's a strategy that...the council is *loathe* to pursue" (emphasis added).

There's at least one respected reference work that says it doesn't make any difference how we spell the italicized word in those sentences, an adjective (when spelled right) meaning strongly reluctant. The suggestion is that we drop the "e" if, in speech, we choose to pronounce it with a hard "th" as in "Goth" or "pith," but use the "e" if we opt for a soft "th," as in "wither" and, well, "loathe," meaning to abhor, to hate.

Fortunately, several other reference works don't go along with that permissiveness. Let the verb be "loathe" and the adjective "loath," however you pronounce them. In this instance, flipping a coin invites a bit of chaos and could drive alert readers crazy.

# Located/Situated

## *Just Being There*

...located at the corner of...

...located near waterways...

...located just across the street from...

The undesirable word is the conspicuous one: "located."

There have long been overly precious arguments against "located" in such contexts — only "situated" is acceptable, the lecture goes — but there's nothing really wrong with it except that we rarely need it. (Any more than we need "situated"; one guess which word was extraneous in "...the marsh behind the house, which was situated about twenty miles west of Portland.")

Both words have a faintly bureaucratic sound, and they don't usually contribute any information.

Occasionally something is needed for balance or rhythm or even sense, as it was in "...strategically located in relation to..." and the nice, easygoing word "placed" would have been perfect.

But most of the time we can just omit "located." We can always wax poetic, of course — sits or lies or perches or squats or rests or is housed or reposes or looms at the corner of...

Then again, we can just omit "located."

# Masterful/Masterly

## *Worth Mastering*

As a verb, "master" can mean to dominate, as with an enemy or an opponent. It also can mean to control skillfully or learn thoroughly, as with a tool or an instrument or a discipline.

For adjectives to cover those two close but distinct ideas we have "masterful" for one who dominates and "masterly" for one who displays skill. Unlike some distinctions born of a horror of having more than one way to say something, this one is useful.

Think "F" for forceful and "masterful" and "L" for lovely and "masterly."

"The junior lefthander pitched a masterful complete-game shutout" certainly made sense. And it was effective to speak of a composer's "masterly command over a wide repertoire."

But the harpist whose playing "was nothing short of masterful" presumably wasn't trying to wrestle the poor harp to the ground.

Not every choice is clear-cut. If that southpaw mixed speeds and enjoyed excellent control in his shutout, he was masterly as well as masterful.

# May/Might

## *I Wish I May...*

"May," as part of a longer verb, puts our thinking in the present — no matter where the rest of the sentence is — and means that at this moment, we're not sure whether something has happened or not.

So sentences like this one don't say what they mean to:

They knew that if they could have somehow played the first half the way they played the second half, they may have won.

That says it's still possible that they won. They didn't, as the sentence makes clear; make it "might have won."

# Media, Plural

## 'Media' Matters

We can skip examples of the use of the word as a singular. They're practically infinite, and maybe the outposts that are holding out for "media" as a plural will be overrun someday. But there are arguments for trying to mount a counterattack.

One has to do with literacy. The word has a useful and much-used singular form, "medium." It came from the Latin into English along with its Latin plural, "media," and both have been established in English since time immemorial. (The Anglicized "mediums" is rare these days, except in reports on the spirit world.) How can "medium" and "media" both be singular? It's not logical, and really not literate, despite those myriad examples of misuse.

Another argument for the plural is philosophical. Public figures — politicians, athletes and their coaches, performers of all kinds — like to blame journalists and journalism for all that isn't wonderful in their lives. They consistently say sneeringly that "the media is" whatever, as if all of us in the ole news game were the same.

Polls that put us down among politicians and used-car salesmen in public esteem suggest that people are buying that notion. But even in a period when traditionally responsible news outlets wallow in sleaze from time to time (and agonize about it), it's unfair to imply that the best and the worst among us are indistinguishable. Subtly, "the media is" does that.

We do well to fight for the plural and to be even clearer by specifying "the news media" when we aren't talking about the trash peddlers or infotainment folks. A subtle counterattack is fair, and literate.

*See also Bacterium/Bacteria; Criterion/Criteria, Phenomenon/Phenomena; and Grafitto/Grafitti*

# Me, Myself (Reflexive Pronouns)

## Call Myself Anytime?

The redoubtable Jane Greer of Bismarck, N.D. (see Reader's Potpourri), sent along some reflections:

> "If you have any questions, contact my secretary or myself." Writers use this because they remember (correctly) from English class that "Bob and me played ball" (where "me" is part of the subject) is wrong, and generalize (incorrectly) that "Give the ball to Bob and me" (where "me" is part of the object of the preposition) must also be wrong — or at least somehow less genteel than "Bob and myself." No, no, no. The "self" words are reflexive pronouns, to be used only when the subject and object of a verb are the same person or thing, as in "I hurt myself" or "He hurt himself" or "The dog hurt itself." Similarly, "Don't hurt yourself" is right because the understood subject, "you," is the same as the object, "yourself." But "I'll send this to Jim and yourself" is wrong; "I" and "yourself" are two different people. The English for it is "to Jim and you."

Speaking of "myself," a note prompted by the discussion in these pages of Older than Him (which see) came from Loren Tretyakov, head of the translation department at the Russian news agency Interfax, where all reports originate in Russian. Noting that her copy editors, native English speakers, often misused pronouns, she went on:

> My contribution is: "'It is assumed that somebody, clearly Primakov and myself are meant, sells Cabinet positions,' he said." Wouldn't "Primakov and I" be correct?

Definitely. Broken down, the clause says that "Primakov is meant and I am meant." What's wanted in such cases is a pronoun that is a subject, in this case "I," not an object. We can't say "myself (or me) is meant," so we have to say "Primakov and I are meant."

*See also "Older than Him"; "To She and I"*

# Missive

See Elegant Variation

# Mondegreens

## *Of Ladies and Colitis*

When this listener's boyhood ears encountered "full of innocence" in Sigmund Romberg's "Student Prince" and recorded the phrase as "full love in a sense," a mondegreen was born. The same thing happened when little Malachy McCourt heard in recitations of the Hail Mary "a monk swimming" instead of "amongst women" (and found himself a title for his memoir in the bargain).

As someone has said, a mondegreen is a sort of a typographical error of the ear. The word was apparently the mid-20th-century brainstorm of a writer named Sylvia Wright. As a child, she heard this couplet from the Scottish ballad "The Bonnie Earl o' Moray"

They ha' slain the Earl o' Moray,
And laid him on the green

and discovered a double murder previously unknown to history — not only the bonnie earl but also the devoted "Lady Mondegreen."

A great word, mondegreen, and apparently grist for a cottage industry; a quick search of the Web can bring hours of happy reading. That's where the classic from the Beatles' "Lucy in the Sky with Diamonds" turned up.

The boys sang hauntingly of "the girl with the kaleidoscope eyes." In the world of mondegreens that became, wondrously, "The girl with colitis goes by."

# Monies

### *Monies? Balonies!*

Public monies would lessen the need to sell so many sponsorships.

On the rare occasion when we need a plural — "the moneys of Central and South America" or some such — the sensible solution is to add an "s" to "money," though dictionaries do include "monies" as an acceptable plural. But as a substitute for plain old "money," or "funds," or "financing"? Leave it to the bureaucrats.

# More Than/Over

### *Dumb and Dumber*

Somewhere along the line, a lot of us were taught that we had to say "more than," and not "over," when dealing with certain amounts. Somebody could be over six feet tall, but we had to say more than ten years.

It's a picky rule — "over" is at least as common as "more than" in literate speech for the relevant situations — and worse than annoying when, as happens often with rules, we follow it out the window. Then we get something like this:

> ...a salary just under $25,000...and well more than Clinton himself would make as attorney general.

Arg. "Well more than" flat-out mangles idiom; nobody *says* anything but "well over." So if we ignore the rule we'll never perpetrate "well more than."

Another lulu born of that silly rule:

> …a hard foul on O'Neal with just more than four minutes to play.

Clank. That four minutes isn't even the kind of thing "more than" is supposed to describe: an amount understood to be counted individually. Four minutes in that sentence is a unit of time, a singular concept. For that reason, as well as to honor idiom, "just over" is the only literate phrasing.

The whole business troubled Doris I. Fenske, an editor in New York with the accounting firm Ernst & Young. She e-mailed to say she was repeatedly running into uses of "over" like this one: "The concert was attended by over 1,000 people." Long ago, she wrote, she was taught to use "more than" in such instances.

> But lately I am seeing "over" everywhere, and my red pen can barely keep up. Am I fighting a losing battle?

It's one that should not have been joined; the rule long foisted on huge numbers of us doesn't make sense. There's nothing wrong with "more than" (assuming we avoid the "well more than" dissonance) but there's nothing wrong with "over," either.

According to *Merriam-Webster's Dictionary of English Usage*, the idea of insisting on "more than" for quantities treated as individually countable sprang full grown from the head of William Cullen Bryant, the poet and journalist, in 1877, when he was editor of the *New York Evening Post*. Bryant apparently gave no explanation for his edict, but journalists picked it up, and taught it, down to our time.

Yet for both countable quantities and round amounts, the dictionary says, "over" has been standard English since the 14th century. All that precedent would seem to make "over" unexceptionable. Better still, natural.

*See also Collective Nouns; They Each; Tons Was.*

# Myriad

## *Lots and Lots, adj. and n.*

A wonderful word, and a strange one, intrigued Kelly Wynne, an undergraduate at the University of Western Sydney, in Australia:

> What is the correct way to use "myriad" — as a noun, with "of" (she was presented with a myriad of options) or as an adjective (she was presented with a myriad options)?

The word, from ancient Greek, originally denoted the number 10,000 and was first used in English only as a noun. It came to refer simply to a very large, indefinite number and to be used as both noun and adjective.

So the answer to Miss Wynne's question is yes on both counts, though with the adjective there seems to be no need for "a."

The choice in this corner is generally to use "myriad" as an adjective and to use it exactly as we'd use "many": She was presented with myriad options.

Or as Longfellow (pleasingly cited in the *American Heritage Dictionary*) put it,

> The forests, with their myriad tongues,
> Shouted of liberty.

# Namesake

## *First, a Name*

Thanks to Nancy Ann Holeman Holmes, an instructor of English at Morris College in South Carolina, for an example of perfectly incorrect use of a pretty common word that is pretty commonly misused.

An article Ms. Holmes read described the secretary of defense at the time, Donald Rumsfeld, as "the namesake of 'Rummyworld,' as Iraq is sometimes referred to..."

That's backward. A namesake is a person or thing named after — in the sake of the name of — another. Joe is the namesake of his grandfather. Mary is her aunt's namesake. And Iraq, when it's called "Rummyworld," is the namesake of Rumsfeld, not the other way around.

It's an easy mistake to make, and keeping the definition pure is worth some effort. Ms. Holmes, asked for help in remembering how it goes, noted that indeed it's a matter of naming *after*:

> The one coming first in time is the "name"; thus, a *namesake* must be the one coming later in time.

Sounds foolproof.

# Native

See 'Former Native'

# Near Miss

## *Almost a Hit*

Jim Benes of WBBM Newsradio 78, Chicago's all-news station, e-mailed to report a running battle — certain morning-drive staff members vs. evening-drive, as it happened — over the phrase "near miss."

The morning people, he said, thought the term could be confusing: "After all, if you nearly miss something, don't you hit it?"

At first blush, "near miss" is a little odd. But it's deeply ingrained in the language. *Merriam-Webster's Dictionary of English Usage,* tracing the phrase to World War II — when it denoted a bomb that caused damage even though it did not score a direct hit — notes its ubiquity and concludes that "despite its apparent lack of logic, it is not an error."

The 1960's edition of *Fowler's Modern English Usage* defines a near miss simply as "a miss that was nearly a hit." The 1994 *Fowler's* omits the phrase, which suggests that it was no longer deemed worthy of discussion.

As an alternative, "near-collision" is unambiguous and unchallengeable. But WBBM's evening-drive cadre was also on target, as it were, with "near miss."

# Neither

## *One Singular or Another*

This, from a newspaper article, contained a wrong number:

> Neither Mr. Bush nor Mr. Gore would say whether they thought...

And so did this, from a sports broadcast:

> Neither team has used their time out.

"Neither," barring complications, conveys a singular idea, whether used with "nor" or by itself. Our first example, after naming two people individually, should have read "whether *he* thought." And our second should have been "*its* time out."

When plural nouns accompany "neither," of course, the plural rules: Neither Porsches nor Cadillacs *appeal* to her; neither *do* Mack trucks.

# None, Plural

## *Think 'Not Any'*

A visitor to the Language Corner Web site, noting that the entry Police, *the*, said at one point, "It's a good bet none of us in journalism do," asked, "Does not 'none' require 'does'?"

More often than not, it doesn't. The word is sometimes used to mean "no one" or "not one," and those are precise ways to say it if we're emphasizing the singular nature of something. But "none" can also denote "not any" and other plural ideas. Its use as a plural is ancient and beyond criticism.

# Normalcy

## *A Word for Parlous Times*

For a little less than four score and seven years, professors and editors have told writers to avoid the word "normalcy." Coined by Warren G. Harding, they said, and what did he know? Only "normality" would do.

But though the great statesman's prescription in his 1920 presidential campaign — "not nostrums, but normalcy" — both popularized the word and drew derision from pedants, "normalcy" had been around long before he used it. Over the years since, says *Merriam-Webster's Dictionary of English Usage*, "normalcy" has become "recognized as standard by all major dictionaries," and "there is no need to avoid its use."

It was hardly avoided after September 11, 2001; it pretty much swamped "normality" to express the condition Americans longed for and whose loss they grieved. And somehow, despite long indoctrination, "normalcy" came to sound perfectly (yes) normal.

# Notoriety

### *Noting with Disapproval*

If "notorious," which has nothing negative in its roots, nonetheless has come to have the very negative meaning "infamous," what is "notoriety"?

One dictionary's definition — "the quality of being notorious" — is circular but hard to argue with. So when the writer said it was "not in Thomas's personality to court notoriety," the passage was open to misunderstanding. Other things made it clear that the aim was a compliment and the word a poor choice.

As a synonym for simple fame or celebrity, "notoriety" has gained ground. But it's still better used to mean a bad reputation: *ill* fame. Less room for misunderstanding.

# Oddities

### *Going with the Flow*

Questions and observations from readers produced a collection whose existence can seem to give logic a bad name.

- Isn't "a friend of mine" a double possessive (which see)? Yes, but idiom loves it and would just hate the alternative, "a friend of me." "A friend of Bob" and "a friend of Bob's," though, are both fine.
- Isn't it wrong to say "six times *more* likely," which might be taken to mean something is 6X *plus* X? Don't we have to say "six times *as* likely"? No. The two are equally well established. Both mean 6X. (But read on; darn.)

- If human beings constitute a species, and a race is a subdivision of a species, how can we talk about the "human race"? Well, writers since Shakespeare — at least — have used the phrase, it is uttered millions of times each day, and there's no going back. (Anyway, "race" at its simplest just means creatures of common origin, which makes it unusually — maddeningly? — flexible.)

None of us who care about the language are immune to twin weaknesses: We hunger for clear-cut rules, and we have a pathological aversion to ambiguity. Sometimes it's best to relax and take what the language gives us.

Within reason, of course...

That all seemed pretty wise until a son with a keen eye and ear for the language (and a math degree) begged to differ in the matter of "six times more." Such phrasing indeed meant 6X plus X, or 7X, he said, to him and to many people he worked with. He later came across supporting evidence in the form of guidelines from a reputable academic organization, though a rather specialized one; those folks "put the 'eek' in 'geek,' " he said.

Further research seemed in order.

*Merriam-Webster's Dictionary of English Usage* acknowledges a certain logic in the 7X view while deriding it. Those who espouse it, the editors declare, are "paying homage to mathematics at the expense of language." And there's more, all sensible.

But the estimable *New York Times Manual of Style and Usage* says "precise readers" might well be 7Xers. Its editors therefore urge the use of "times as much (or as fast, etc.)."

So, a smart kinsman, some solid geeks, and an industry standard on usage (differing from another) — not to mention the newspaper editor who raised the question with Language Corner in the first place — all saying "6 times more than X" means "7X."

Most readers, including an awful lot of precise ones, clearly don't see the world that way. But the hardy few aren't nit-picking cranks, their numbers are more than infinitesimal, and they can't be ignored. "Six times more" is pretty much unusable.

A sad state of affairs? Perhaps. But "six times as much as X" and just "six times X" are idiomatic, unambiguous, a reasonable compromise, and a safer bet.

## Off of

See Fused Participle

## Of Which

See Whose/Of Which

## 'Older than Him'; 'To She and I'
### *Do We Have an Understanding?*

Sometimes sentences have to be written with words that are not seen but are understood to be there. The ones in which "you" is understood — "[You] Come to dinner!" — are the most common examples. This was another:

His brother John, who is five years older than him, and George, who is three years older than him, both became doctors.

Even in casual conversation, that's illiterate (quite apart from the need for the plural "brothers"). The reason is a little word that doesn't appear: "is."

What the writer meant to say is that the brothers were five and three years "older than he is." So make it "older than he" or, less stiltedly, "older than he is." But never, unless obliged to quote illiterate speech precisely, "older than him."

The error can arise in the plural, too:

> They have found a team as dysfunctional and foolish as them.

The word "are" being understood, the sentence has to read "...as they." Or better yet, "as they are."

On a similar matter, Margery Simmons of Orlando, Fla., from a family "replete with teachers," e-mailed to express annoyance with "the now prevalent use of the wrong case for pronouns in prepositional phrases," adding, "I have the feeling that I would still be in eighth grade if I had said, "...gave it to she and I.""

Eighth grade (or earlier) is when we ought to have learned that the pronouns that are used as subjects — I, we, he, she, they, who — can't be used as objects. In this case "she and I" are objects of the preposition "to." Probably no English-speaker would ever write or say "to she," but somehow people do write things like "to she and I." Two wrongs don't make a right. The right way, of course, is "to her and me."

In another age, rumor has it, Americans got a lot of their entertainment from radio serials. One of the longtime favorites was "The Aldrich Family," whose teenaged son, Henry, was fond of the pronoun "I" — "Are you calling I, Mother?" "He wants to talk with I?" Henry thought it sounded elegant, but Henry could be a pretty dumb kid.

*See also Me, Myself (Reflexive Pronouns).*

# One in Four: Singular

## *A Plural Trap*

An American working as a copy editor abroad, who did not want to be identified further, e-mailed to ask,

> Which headline would be correct: "1 In 4 Americans Chew Sugarless Gum" or "1 In 4 Americans Chews Sugarless Gum"?

The second phrasing is correct. The subject of the verb is as singular as can be — 1 — so the verb has to be singular, too: "chews." It's not "Americans" (all of them, or even four of them) doing the chewing. It's one American, out of (in this case) four.

Such constructions, even when correct, are often a little awkward. A slightly more relaxed approach would be "1 American in 4 Chews Sugarless Gum" — 1...chews.

A similar puzzle with a different answer is in the following entry.

# One Of/Among with Plural Verb

## *A Singular Trap*

Because it contains a very common kind of error, this passage seemed worthy of comment:

> ...the Catskill OTB is among the few parlors that does not record calls.

An e-mail cemented the choice of topic.

Neil T. Greenidge of the Bronx, a physician and a member of the class of 1962 at the Columbia University School of General Studies, wrote, "I did not expect such a glaring, though universal, grammatical error from CU," his alma mater.

He was talking about this, from the *Columbia Journalism Review:*

> The *Atlantic,* one of the few American magazines that still dares to publish high-quality, complex narratives...

Dr. Greenidge was absolutely right. Both passages lay a trap. They induce us to allow a singular notion — "the Catskill OTB" and "The *Atlantic,* one of the few" — to carry us past what follows, straight to a singular verb.

But what follows is critical. The verbs in both cases should be plural, because the noun that governs each of them is plural. It's parlors that do not record calls, and magazines that still dare to publish.

We — the pronoun is especially apt here — need to be alert. The slip happens all the time. (And sometimes it's no slip; some authorities argue for the singular verb. The argument defies logic.)

The *New York Times Manual of Style and Usage* suggests a little test: Turn such sentences around to see how the elements really work. That would give us "Among the few parlors that do not record calls, one is the Catskill OTB" and "Of the few American magazines that still dare to publish high-quality, complex narratives, the *Atlantic* is one." (A test — only a test. But a valid test.)

"Enjoyed the article," Dr. Greenidge said at the end of his e-mail, and so did we all. The author deserved better from his editors, especially from the last one to read the copy in each issue, who is expected to catch such slips. He wrote this little essay while kicking himself, which isn't easy to do.

# 'One of the Only'

## Not *the Only Way to Go*

Over a decade or so, half a dozen people e-mailed Language Corner seeking support for their campaign to stamp out "one of the only." "Only" means "one," darn it, and you can't have one of the one, and so on; the only option is "one of the few."

That view is widely held, but to this student it's overly picky — one of those times when a tiny germ of logic, discovered under a microscope, grabs hold and won't let go. (For an extreme example of that process, see Possessive Nouns with Pronouns.)

"Only" attaches comfortably to all kinds of plural ideas: "Only three things matter in this world" and the like. And "one of the only," with its suggestion of rarity — fewer than "few" — conveys a meaning the other phrase doesn't.

If we can say — as of course we can — "Pierre's and Moulin Rouge are the only French restaurants in town," how can we prohibit "Pierre's is one of the only French restaurants in town"? Or argue with a hurricane-damage chronicler who reported, as one did after Katrina and Rita in 2005, "It was one of the only unlooted stores in the Quarter"?

"One of the only" is reasonable and well established. But it annoys some commentators mightily, so beware.

"If I didn't know better," one e-mail friend said, winding up a detailed polemic, "I would suspect you had been sucked into some sort of payola scheme. Were an open bar and karaoke involved, by any chance?"

It never happened!

Well, a bottle of Beefeater's at Christmas, maybe...

Nothing, of course, keeps those who hate "one of the only" from restricting themselves to "one of the few," which is only slightly more vague.

*See also None, Plural.*

## Only, Placement Of

### *Only Where It Belongs*

A mong the many things that are natural in conversation among literate people but don't pass muster in writing is the misplacement of "only."

In conversation, this would have been utterly natural and instantly understandable:

> In the past, agents have only testified about their procedures and activities.

But that sentence was in the public prints, where the voice can't be heard and the requirements are stricter.

"Only" is happiest, most of the time, snug up against what it modifies. The writer didn't mean the agents only testified — as opposed, for example, to chatting or singing or praying. "Only" had to do with what they testified about: procedures and activities.

The sentence would have been instantly clear and perfectly comfortable had it said the agents "have testified only about their procedures and activities." (The letter of the law might call for "testified about only their procedures and activities," but that's a bit clumsy.)

## Onomatopoeia

See 'Woof Down'

# Oral/Verbal

## *Of Tongue or Pen*

A reader on the Web, whose identification data were unfortunately lost in the ether, called attention to this indignity:

> A recent news report included the following phrase: "despite her written and verbal instructions…" Like many people the writer did not understand that the words "verbal" and "oral" do not mean the same thing. Verbal instructions can be both oral and written.

But the context usually makes the meaning clear, and this one did too, right? Maybe; probably. But leaving such things to chance is sloppy.

"Oral" means "spoken," and vice versa (rather than written), and that's probably what the writer of the cited passage had in mind. "Verbal," not just literally but also as a practical matter, means using words any which way except…what? Body language? Smoke signals?

If we mean to refer to speech to the exclusion of the written word, "oral" and "spoken" do so precisely.

# Orient/Orientate

## *Trouble to the East?*

Seth Wigderson, an American sojourning at the University of Manitoba, e-mailed about "an old question which I have never seen resolved: Is the verb 'orient' or 'orientate'?"

Surprisingly and redundantly, it's both. A number of dictionaries include "orientate," along with "orient," to mean to get one's bearings, literally or figuratively; to align something with points of the compass; or (by the root meaning "east") to put in place facing east.

Why we have "orientate" is anybody's guess; it tends to look like a mistake. Could the noun "orientation" have suggested it? Seems likely. Nobody says represent or experimentate, but pool players, lining up an extra carom, have been known to announce that they were going to "combinate off the six ball."

As it happens, Mr. Wigderson's question arose from encounters with "orientate" in the United States. He might well have run into it even more often in Canada, since it's apparently more popular in the many realms of British English.

But it's not preferable, and certainly not required, anywhere. Mr. Wigderson noted that he preferred "orient." That is emphatically the preference here, too.

# 'Paint the Lily'

See Gild/Paint the Lily

# Partake/Participate/Take Part
## *Many Parts to Play*

"Partake" and "take part" and "participate" don't all mean the same thing. They're siblings, but not clones. It's usually "partake" that we mangle:

> ...just another roadblock to people partaking in elections

> ...the audience can partake in the same way

> ...one of 50 hunters selected to partake in the...hunt

All of those wanted some form of "take part" or "participate," meaning to assume a role or a function in something.

To partake is to enjoy — often by eating — a portion of something. And notice these prepositions: We take part or participate "in," but we partake "of." For example,

> They can partake of a thick lamb stew...

Sometimes any of the siblings can play, depending on the preposition. (Wouldn't it be nice if we had more absolutes?) A published passage read, "He can partake in his three favorite hobbies," and that was off the mark. But "partake of" would have made it work, with only an ignorable difference in meaning.

# People/Persons

See Individuals/People/Persons

# Per

### *English Preferred*

There was no mortal sin here:

> Updated continually, with new content five days per week...

But why use Latin? "Per," here and very often, reads like corporate memo-ese. The English "five days a week" is much more natural. Similarly, "miles an hour" is the natural phrasing, despite the standard abbreviation MPH. Does anybody, in conversation, ever say "miles per hour"?

Latin is lovely; English couldn't do without it. And "per" has its place because there are times when "a" or "for each" just doesn't work. But we ought at least to think twice before abandoning vernacular English. Even in corporate memos.

# Percentage Increases and Decreases

See Five Times Below, 160% Less, etc.

# Persons

See Individuals/People/Persons

# Phenomenon/Phenomena

See Criterion/Criteria

# 'Pleaded Guilty'

### *A Modest Plea*

The bank, a news article reported, "had pled guilty to charges that it made false entries."

Why "pled"? A lot of lawyers (and a lot of lawyerly writings) seem to prefer it, and some dictionaries list it as an alternative past tense for "plead." But we don't say someone "pled for his life" or "pled for mercy"; we say "pleaded." And so it should be with legal pleas. Case closed, one hopes.

But no, not quite closed, and fair enough. Drew Trott, a staff attorney at the Sixth District Court of Appeal in San Jose, Calif., saw those thoughts on the Web and was doubtful. He e-mailed to say he had looked in the ultra-comprehensive *Oxford English Dictionary* and found quite a few examples of "pled," starting with Edmund Spenser in 1596. For himself, Mr. Trott said he not only used the word and ran into it in both formal and informal contexts but also found it more pleasing to the ear than "pleaded":

> I suspect it is for similar reasons that we don't say "readed,"
> "bleeded" or "speeded" — they are unpoetic…I acknowledge
> that we lawyers do say "deeded," but in that instance, consider
> the alternative.

Aha! A point well taken. And more research seemed essential.

The *O.E.D.* traces "pled" to Scottish legal usage and dialect. The
dictionary's citations are balanced, and those for "pleaded," by
gum, include Blackstone, the giant of Western law.

Several references call "pled" colloquial, but a couple say it is established American usage. If so, it doesn't seem frequent in any kind
of formal writing, and the American press certainly isn't sympa-
thetic to it. A Nexis search turned up "pleaded" overwhelmingly.

That result is probably skewed, however. The Associated Press
stylebook, the guide on such matters for most American newspapers, condemns "pled" as colloquial. And the *New York
Times* stylebook, also influential, prescribes "pleaded" without
comment.

There may be room for argument, and "pled" may be gaining.
It is certainly not irrational for the ear to prefer it to "pleaded."
But the strong preference here, and clearly the safer course in
American journalistic writing early in the 21st century, remains
"pleaded."

# Pole/Post Position

## *Off to the Races*

A couple of e-mail visitors thought the entry called Series:
Changing Numbers (which see) was incorrect in referring to
the "post positions," plural, in a horse race.

They were influenced by auto racing, in which the inside position in the front rank of cars on the track is called the "pole position."

In Thoroughbred racing, which the cited article referred to, each stall in the starting gate is a post position — No. 1 being closest to the inside rail or hedge, No. 2 second closest, and so on.

Although all kinds of things influence the outcomes of all kinds of races, both the pole position and the No. 1 post position have a certain advantage starting out. This was an interesting figurative application:

> With years of experience at every stage of the process, Brazil is in the pole position to help other nations' farmers grow crops...

Probably not written by a horseplayer.

# Police, *the*

## *You've Got to Be Carefully Taught*

Practically everybody in journalism writes or broadcasts it this way: "Police said Mrs. Guerin..." and "Police say there is little doubt..." Practically nobody in the real world talks that way. (As a language-maven friend noted, we'd never say, "Army said." Why "police said"?)

It's a good bet none of us in journalism say such things, either, when we're not reading a script. We say, "She called *the* police," or "*The* police said." Why? Because it's natural English. Dropping "the" is unnatural, something all of us news people had to learn as young adults — brisk writing, or something. But ain't nature grand?

*See also Have to/Got to.*

# Possessives, Double

See Double Possessive (I and II)

# Possessive Nouns with Pronouns
## *A Rule to Ignore*

A lot of attention was devoted not long ago to a grammar argument, of all things, between a high school journalism teacher and the College Board. The teacher won.

He had objected to this part of a sentence on the Preliminary Scholastic Aptitude Test (PSAT) administered in 2002:

> Toni Morrison's genius enables her...

The teacher insisted — for three months — that a possessive noun (Toni Morrison's) functions as an adjective and can't lead logically to a pronoun (her). In late May 2003, the College Board capitulated, as in fairness it had to. Such a rule did show up in a few grammar books, so students who applied it couldn't be penalized.

The triumphant teacher, clearly a dedicated man, was roundly cheered. Yet the rule that enticed him years ago defies common sense.

Must "Jane's word is her bond" become "Jane's word is Jane's bond"? No. Possessives with their very own pronouns have been ubiquitous in good English writing forever. Avoiding them is tortured. (Quick checks of Shakespeare [*Julius Caesar*], Dickens [*David Copperfield*], and, indeed, Morrison [*Beloved*] turned up, not at all surprisingly, exactly such usage.)

After the College Board surrendered, the Stanford linguist Geoffrey Nunberg, writing in the *New York Times,* provided legal support, as it were, for sense and universal usage. Possessives like "Toni Morrison's," he said, should be thought of not as adjectives but as "determiner phrases," which can be tied to pronouns. Nice to know, but if we need such crutches we're in trouble.

Earlier, one commentator savaged the board, saying it "wrote an error" into the PSAT. His solution: Say "The genius of Toni Morrison...," making the name work as a noun, leading legally to "her." Well, all English possessives can be formed with "of," and not always happily. Anybody care for "The word of Jane is her bond"? Try tapping to the rhythm of "The body of John Brown lies a-mouldering in the grave, but his soul goes marching on."

It's nonsense.

The apostrophe is so handy. French speakers have to make do with "la plume de ma tante," but English speakers can say "my aunt's pen." And we can certainly add, "is mightier than her sword."

*See also Antecedents.*

# Precipitate/Precipitous

See Evoke/Invoke

# Preposition Ending Sentence

## The Way of All Flesh

I reviewed my list of friends and acquaintances and established that there was not a single one of them whom I could drop in on. (In on whom I could drop? No matter.)

Right — no matter. Ending a sentence with a preposition can sometimes be clumsy, but so can a lot of things. In general, for most good writers, the rule against it was long since repealed.

And so the television commentator got the who/whom right — "He is the best type of pitcher against whom to hit-and-run" — but something he learned in junior high inhibited him. The sentence is much more natural if it reads "...pitcher to hit-and-run against."

Winston Churchill is supposed to have declaimed, "There are some things up with which I will not put." A bit of derision the rest of us can profit from.

# Prior to/Before

## *Prior Offense*

That's the way to use "prior" — as an adjective. As a preposition, "prior to" is very close to non-English, however widespread.

> Prior to 1965, virtually no one was speaking of abortion as a prospective right.

What in heaven's name is wrong with "before"? We don't have to follow the lead of such folk as football referees, who invariably say, "False start, prior to the snap..." Or of the academics, doctors, lawyers, and bureaucrats of all stripes, public and private, for whom "prior to" is mandatory because "before" is plain English, and they can't have *that*.

Fowler, in his *Dictionary of Modern English Usage,* tolerated "prior to," rather puzzlingly, in cases where the connection between two events is "more essential than the simple time relation" but otherwise consigned it to the dread category of Formal Words, along with "following" as a substitute for "after." From this seat, "following" sometimes seems useful in connoting immediacy or causality, but that may be a character flaw. And using it may encourage such extremes as this, from a television sports announcer:

> Immediately following the conclusion of tonight's broadcast...

Deposing on after/following and before/prior to in his delightfully erudite book *Words on Words,* the late John Bremner, a legendary teacher of journalism at the University of Kansas, asked,

If you don't use posterior to, why use prior to? Would you say "Posterior to the game, we had a few drinks"? So why say, "Prior to the game, we had a few drinks"? Make it: "Before and after (and even during) the game, we had a few drinks."

We can all drink to that.

# Problematic

See Fulsome/Problematic

# Rage/Wage
## *The Sin of Wages*

First one pop performer and then another, Curtis Gropp reported in an e-mail to Language Corner, insisted on singing "But the battle wages on for toy soldiers." Irritating, but Gropp, a copywriter for Creative Ad Services in Huntington Beach, Calif., just assumed it was a one-song slipup.

Then some impulse made him check. Sure enough, there on the Web he encountered "Custody battle wages on" and "Spam wars: The battle wages on" and many other such fanciful uses of "wage."

A twanscwibed speech impediment?

As Mr. Gropp noted, "wage" means to engage in, conduct, carry out. It's a transitive verb, meaning it must have an object — we have to "wage" *something* — a battle, a campaign, war. "Wage," by itself, just doesn't work, with or without "on."

"Rage," by itself, does. It's an intransitive verb, not allowed to have a direct object. Whatever or whoever is raging just does what "rage" means — proceed or spread violently, or blow off steam — without doing it *to* anything else. No one can rage war or a campaign or a battle or a storm. Those things (among others) just "rage" by themselves. Or sometimes "rage on."

# Ravage/Ravish

## *Weather Has Its Limits*

The interesting word "ravish" got a lot of inappropriate play in the aftermath of the great hurricanes of 2005. We read of the "migration of humanity from storm-ravished areas" and of "a school ravished by Hurricane Katrina" and learned that a musician's "mobile home was ravished."

In those examples, the desired word was "ravaged." It means to seriously damage or destroy, as the storms did so terribly on the Gulf Coast. Think "age" for damAGE and ravAGE.

"Ravish" means to rape, in both the narrow sexual sense and the sense of to seize or take away by force; a critic aptly described a wacky movie character who "crawls on the pavement...while begging them to ravish her..."

In another sense, "ravish" means to enrapture, or transport in delight, and provides the verbal adjective "ravishing," meaning entrancing or beautiful in a sensual way:

> some of the most ravishing soft singing
>
> the ravishing Florentine girl who inspired Dante...

Not, one hopes, in a damaging or destructive way.

# Raveled Sleeve, with an 'A'

## *Brush Up Your Shakespeare, Act III*

Find the misspelling:

> Sleep, as Shakespeare wrote, knits up the raveled sleeve of care.

No, not "raveled," though it can be spelled with two "l's." The error, a very frequent one, is "sleeve."

Macbeth wasn't talking about the arm of a garment; that wouldn't really make sense. He was talking about a tangled skein, of silk or other material, and that makes perfect sense. And for that, the spelling — which the original author used, of course — is "sleave."

It's an obsolete word now, but spelling it right is still the right move. Many readers may dismiss it as just another typo (a Nexis search shows it's a frequent typo for "sleeve"), but those who know better will smile. You'll have to ignore your spell-checker, though.

*Other matters Shakespearean appear in Gild/Paint the Lily; Honored in the Breach; and Wherefore.*

# A Reader's Potpourri

## *The Buzz It Buzzeth*

After a few e-mail exchanges, Jane Greer of Bismarck, N.D., who "commits public relations for a major Midwestern ad agency," but only after "what seemed to be a lifetime in state government," sent along a hefty collection of things that get under her skin, and should. A sampling follows, in her own words.

## Implement

This word has dozens of subtly different meanings that generally stand for either "start" or "accomplish," but we all "implement." Why?

## Interface

An interface, among other things, is the connection between a computer program and its user. Non-techies have come to use it as a verb meaning "talk with each other." I don't get it.

## Share

You're welcome to share your inheritance with me, but not your feelings. This word is used without thought by folks to mean they're going to tell me something. Don't try to make me feel warm and fuzzy. Just tell me what you want to tell me.

## Utilize

Of all the bad habits American speakers and writers have, this one seems hardest to break. Too many people who should know better still write and say "utilize" in place of good old "use." The fancier word shouldn't be banned — one worthwhile definition is "to turn to profitable account or use" — but usually all people gain by using it is two syllables and the joy of feeling superior when in fact they sound ridiculous. ("Utilization" is even more abominable.) Let's not let our language make us look foolish. That's what car phones are for.

*See also Me, Myself.*

# The Reason Is *That*

### *Reason Enough*

> Mr. Dole asserted that the reason his proposal had yet to catch on was because media coverage of it had been overwhelmingly negative.

Make it "the reason was...that..." Why? Because...the sense of "because" is already in the sentence in the word "reason," and if we use "because" we're repeating ourselves. That's unattractively tautological.

To which Joseph C. Alvarez, describing himself as a retired Air Force man and a "fiddler," responded by e-mail with a variation on the theme:

> I submit that "why" grates on my nerves when used after "the reason..." It is smoother and neater simply to say, "The reason he failed to make himself clear, etc."

"Theirs not to reason why," Tennyson wrote. But he was using "reason" as a verb, and the memorable line was also logical. The "why" that irks Mr. Alvarez shows up often and rarely serves a purpose.

*See also Tautology.*

# Rebut/Refute

### In Rebuttal

The team was waiting to hear what would happen to sexual-assault accusations against one of its members, the article and headline reported. The bank of the headline said,

> No charges yet as teammate refutes woman's claim.

The accused player hadn't yet refuted anything; there had been no finding on the truth of the charges.

The word is stronger than "rebut," with which it's often confused. "Refute" means to disprove, conclusively. "Rebut" means simply to deny, or present argument against, an allegation. And more than half the time, "deny" will get the job done more naturally than "rebut."

# Refer

See Allude/Refer

# Reference as a Verb

### Bureaucratic Direction

A database search confirms the impression that the unattractive use of "reference" as a verb has grown exponentially in the last years of the old century and the early years of the new one.

The verb has been around a long time in the phrase "cross reference," and it has some specialized applications of its own (a textbook that is well referenced, for instance). But mostly it's business and legal jargon — you know, the above referenced quadruple ax murder — and should be shunned by English-speakers.

It was painful to read

- about "communal tables referencing a monastery or a refectory"
- that a governor wrote his legislators "a letter referencing the Rolling Stones"
- that a writer "referenced Montaigne" and that a speaker "referenced the old parable: pride goes before the fall."

And how excuse the claim that a fashion designer's work "referenced Ibsen and Strindberg"?

"Reference" probably showed up in those passages for two reasons, neither happy. First, its very sloppiness makes it handy (as with the ubiquitous "facility," which see). We don't have to search for anything that really *fits* because "reference" fits all. Second, like others of its tin-eared ilk, "reference" has caught on because it seems fashionable. For some reason, bureaucratese invites imitation. Maybe syllables impress.

But in fact "reference" is a poor substitute for the many words and phrases that do fit. Those tables *evoked*; the governor *invoked*; the writer *cited*; the speaker *quoted*; the designer's work *evoked*, perhaps, or *recalled the age of*.

Suggest, speak of, call to mind, allude, mention — all put "reference" to shame. Not to mention little old "refer."

# Referendum(s)

See Graffiti/Graffito

# Reflexive Pronouns

See Me, Myself

# Refute

See Rebut/Refute

# Regard/Regards

### *A Regard? Take Two*

A friend and former *Columbia Journalism Review* colleague, the journalist and Web wizard Wendy Bryan, e-mailed from her new post in Los Angeles with a question from a friend of hers:

> Is "with regards to" correct, or is it always "with regard to"? And even more pressing: Are regards given only to Broadway?

Well, sort of; no; and not necessarily.

"Regards" with an "s," is fine if we're talking about warm thoughts, the sort George M. Cohan was sending to Broadway. But that means that "with regards to" seems to work only at the end of a letter, as in "With regards to Aunt Mary, Love, Ignace."

"With regards to" is definitely not fine as a phrase meaning "concerning" or "in reference to." For that, idiom insists on "with (or in) regard to" — no "s." But wait: What about "as regards"? Alas, it needs the "s" and means the same as "in regard to." No getting around it, annoying as it is. And let's not forget "regarding."

Finally, with regard to "regards" and Broadway, a little-known gem of Tin Pan Alley lore: Cohan first wrote the witty and sophisticated "Give My Regards to the Gowanus Canal," but he could never find a publisher.

# Reluctant/Reticent

## *In Other Words, Shy*

The article spoke of a company's "reticence to sign further contracts at that time." It should have spoken of the company's "reluctance."

Reticence is only one form of reluctance. And the words work differently.

"Reticence" means reluctance to speak up or come forward; silence; reserve. (Think reTIring, reTIcence.) And along with its adjective, "reticent," our word is commonly followed by a word or phrase meaning "concerning": His reticence *about* the accounts made the investigators suspicious.

Like "silence" or "reserve," "reticence" is uncomfortable with an infinitive; "reticence to sign," or "to" do anything, will offend every time. "Reluctance" and "reluctant," though, work nicely with infinitives, as for example in "reluctance to sign further contracts at that time."

# Remunerate/Renumerate

## *Think M, as in Money*

...a military career remains popular in part because an officer's renumeration is better...

With better renumeration for doctors, it is natural...

...the salary would be a drop in the renumerations bucket.

"Renumeration," reasonable as it may look, has no place in those passages. What's wanted is "remuneration," with the "m" first, not the "n."

"Remuneration" is often just a fancy word for "pay," as it seems to be in the first example. But the word is usable when we need to cover other forms of reward — bonuses and stock options, anyone? — as in that "bucket."

The reversing of the consonants — "num" instead of the correct "mun" — is puzzling. But it is fairly common, especially, it seems, in outlets of the British sort.

Some of us (he confessed) used to think "renumerate," along with its presumed noun, "renumeration," wasn't a word at all. Alas, it is, though many dictionaries omit it and it's neither pretty nor widely used. It means to enumerate — list one by one — again; count over.

# Replete

## *More than Complete*

"Replete with," a phrase that seems to go through cycles of popularity in journalism, is often used incorrectly to mean just "having" or "equipped with."

In fact, it means having an abundance or a surfeit. A ten-acre estate with one swimming pool is pretty standard stuff; the estate comes complete with pool. The same spread with eight pools would be replete with them.

The writer who told of "a ludicrous erotic 'Slap That Bass,' replete with tacky bumps and grinds" got it right.

But a weakness for fancy-sounding words seemed to be at work with a basketball team that was "replete with colorful coach and mid-major charm" and a "toolbox, replete with hammer, tape measure and plane level."

# Resonate

## *Heard Enough?*

Unlike the distinctly unlovely use of "reference" as a verb (which see) the figurative use of "resonate" is effective and apt. But like "reference," it became painfully popular as the centuries rolled over; a nice metaphor has been cheapened.

"Resonate" means to sound strongly and deeply, or to echo, pleasingly or otherwise:

> It is a sound created in the larynx; it resonates in the chest.

And our word makes for a fine, versatile metaphor, meaning ring a bell, strike a chord, make a strong impression, have a lasting impact, be memorable, and so on. And on.

> But it takes a Byrne, Rushdie or Fellini or Dali to make the details resonate.
>
> What is important is that the Teen-age Mutants resonate so strongly with the kids
>
> The very name of their initial base, at Quonset Point, R.I., would soon resonate across the Pacific.
>
> The songs…resonate to her own experience.
>
> When people see the big company letterhead, it resonates well.

Maybe not *that* versatile.

But enough — and that's the point. It's trite. We should let it rest awhile.

# Restrictive Clause

See That/Which

# Reverend

## *Nouns, for Heaven's Sake!*

An actress's obituary said she had once played "the conflicted daughter of a Bible-wielding reverend." Maybe the writer and editor were having fun; if so, the signals weren't clear, and they have to be.

"Reverend," as a noun meaning a member of the clergy, is colloquial at best, and used with a straight face borders on the illiterate. Some dictionaries include the noun definition, some without even a frown, and the forces of darkness may be gaining, as in a published headline bank that spoke of "remarks...made by the reverend."

But the word is an adjective, an honorific that properly takes "the" — "the Reverend John Smith," or more usually in journalism, with the full name, "the Rev." Common nouns for such people include priest, rabbi, minister, preacher, clergyman or clergywoman, imam, and pastor. In any case, let's stick to nouns. "Reverend" isn't part of that flock.

The spirit moved Bob Pounds, a public affairs officer at the Australian Department of Veterans' Affairs in Canberra, to send along these thoughts (he's sure there's also a six-line version) on matters clerical:

> Call me Brother if you will,
> Pastor, Teacher, better still,
> Minister, clergyman, counselor, friend.
> Just never call me Reverend.

Amen.

# Sequence of Tenses

### The Present as Past

Ian Edwards, an information officer with the Organization of American States in Washington, wanted to know whether it is correct to write "...the president said that America is the lone superpower." Should "is" be there in the present tense, or should it be "was"?

The question opens (briefly) a can of worms called "sequence of tenses."

Within any sentence or other discrete block of writing, it's usually better to abide by the tense that brung ya. "The president said that America was" — "said," past tense, followed by "was," past tense — is always acceptable. The president said it in the past and it applied, strictly speaking, only to that moment. "Was" can never be wrong in such circumstances. "She said she was [not is] confused" is clearly the best choice for that thought, for example.

Mr. Edwards's question, though, involves an exception that proves the rule: If a statement applies to a continuing condition, even if only in the speaker's mind, it's usually preferable to let the present tense follow the past. "He said women are [not were] generally paid less than men for the same work" passes that test. So does "She insisted that the moon is [not was] made of green cheese." So does "The president said that America is [not was] the lone superpower."

Similarly, it's safest to move from one tense to another in a strictly logical sequence: "The president said he had decided not to act" — "said," in the past tense, followed by "had decided," past perfect, for something previous to the saying for which no time is specified in the sentence.

But if the time of the decision is specified, the simple past again asserts itself: "The president said he decided Wednesday not to act." Using "had decided" in that one would change the meaning subtly and make it incorrect. With "had" the sentence would say — speaking very technically, now — that by Wednesday the president's decision was already in the past.

# Series: Changing Numbers

## *One Was, Two Were*

"The field was set and post positions drawn," the article about horse racing said, and that was a numbers slip, so to speak. The error is easy to spot in a series consisting of just "field" and "post positions"; not so easy to spot, and easier to commit, as series grow longer.

The noun "field" in the first part of the sentence is singular, and of course works fine with the singular "was set." But "positions" in the next part of the sentence is plural, and the singular "was" from the beginning of the sentence no longer applies. That means "drawn" is only half a verb.

The sentence has to read, "The field was set and post positions were drawn."

What if the number — singular or plural — in such a series stays the same from beginning to end? Then the auxiliary verb can be omitted (though that's not mandatory) with the second and subsequent elements:

Post positions were drawn, weights assigned and jockeys named.

And we're off!

*See also Pole/Post Position.*

# Series, Run-On

## *Serial Comment*

There was a small but frequent goof here:

Ochoa had two singles, a double and scored twice.

There's a series in that sentence. It's governed by the verb "had," and it consists of only two things: Ochoa's hits.

135

The rest of the sentence is a new clause, with the understood subject "he" (for "Ochoa") and its own verb, "scored"; "had" is out of the picture. So it should read "Ochoa had two singles *and* a double and scored twice." When the verb changes, be alert.

It's not always a verb that governs, though. Here, it's an adjective:

> ...107 delegates from every state, territory and the District of Columbia.

"Every" governs only the two-part series consisting of "state" and "territory"; it can't be used to modify "District of Columbia." The sentence has to read "state *and* territory and the District of Columbia."

Again,

> ...an elaborate script...used mainly for monograms, engravings, and on the menus of fancy restaurants.

Spend the three letters; put "and" after "monograms" (the second and last part of the series linked to "for").

There seems to be a reflexive resistance to repeating "and" in such situations. But it's essential to note the word or phrase that governs a series — "had" for Ochoa's performance, "every" for the origins of those delegates, "for" for the first two places that script shows up — and to make sure it works with *everything* that comes after. If not, we need to start a fresh thought.

# Serve/Service

## *Avoiding Service*

A note from Carl Czech, who works for the Navy in Coronado, Calif., was both indignant and eloquent:

> I find myself wincing when people describe the act of "servicing customers." I often hear variations of the phrase applied to work on behalf of clients, subordinates, or other constituents. I've

always used "serve" to describe such relationships. While I'm apt to have a mechanic service my car, it's only when I'm overcharged that I feel personally "serviced."

That last feeling, no doubt, stems from the (correct) use of "service" as a verb to describe the performance of a stallion with a mare.

Though the lines seem to be blurring, "serve" is usually what people do for those "clients, subordinates, or other constituents." A waiter serves patrons in a restaurant; a railroad serves many communities; a sales rep serves a dozen clients (in practice, that one may be a close call).

"Service," the verb, essentially a coinage of the automobile age, best describes the supply, maintenance, and repair of machinery, equipment, vehicles, vessels, and the like. It also refers to the payment of interest on debt. And it is an accepted term in animal breeding, which is why it can sometimes sound pretty silly when applied to human interactions.

# Shakespeare

Some frequently abused citations appear in Gild/Paint the Lily; Honored in the Breach; Raveled Sleave, with an 'A'; and Wherefore.

# Share

See Reader's Potpourri

# Singular Noun, Plural Pronoun

## *There's No 'They' There*

The article paraphrased an official as saying that "no bond firm should feel any pressure simply because they were called by the City Budget Director." Another piece said that "the network is looking to change all that by following their old letters with a new number: 24."

At least so far, a bond firm isn't a "they," it's an "it." And the possessive pronoun for a network is "its," not "their." Singular, not plural.

In conversation we all use the plural "they" and "them" after singular nouns, and no one (except maybe the colleague who was the smartest kid in the fifth grade) would consider correcting us out loud. In writing, though, the use of the plural should be avoided; it's still almost universally considered wrong in American English. If the singular pronoun sounds too forced, reworking the passage is worth the effort.

The day may come when "they" is accepted as a reference to both singular and plural antecedents, but it hasn't come yet.

*See also He or She, etc.*

# Situated

See Located/Situated

# Sleight/Slight of Hand

## *Not from the Latin*

Part of the glory and much of the quirkiness of English stem from the number of places where the language started life. These passages confused a word from Old Norse with a word from Middle Dutch:

> a little legislative slight-of-hand and deck-stacking
>
> thrown into noncompliance with the law by this slight of hand
>
> take a bit of Shakespeare, stir in a magician's slight of hand

The word that was wanted in those examples was "sleight," from an Old Norse word for cunning or sly. "Sleight" means deftness or skill, or a deft or skillful act. The word is pretty much confined these days to the expression "sleight of hand," a magician's deception and by extension slick tricks of all sorts.

On the other hand (as it were) "slight" is thought to have emerged from Middle Dutch for simple or plain. It means, of course, small or not much: a slight person, slight intelligence. As a verb, "slight" means to neglect or pay scant attention to.

Why do we need two words pronounced "slite"? Because they arrived, they stayed, and here we are, after all that time.

# 'Snuck'

## *Creeping Up*

A couple of pen pals of this collection — Mark W. Freeman (see Wangle/Wrangle) and Nancy Ann Holeman Holmes (see Namesake) — independently and almost simultaneously brought up the subject of the past tense of "sneak."

Both were offended by "snuck," which seemed to be showing up more and more in the public prints, and their aversion was justified. But a light dawned: In conversation, pretty much invariably, the unthinking choice of this traveler was — "snuck."

The written language is apparently not ready for it, though. Most authorities still consider "sneaked" standard. But can that last?

"Snuck," of mysterious but apparently 19th-century American origin, is ubiquitous in speech, is more common by the day in both humorous and serious writing, and even shows up in some dictionaries as an alternative past tense and participle.

An unstoppable wave? It may well be. But "sneaked" isn't going to disappear anytime soon. So unless we're playing around, it's the safer choice.

# Split Infinitive

## *Splitsville*

Splitting an infinitive is not a grave offense, but it's nice to avoid because it makes some grammarians and other thoughtful readers — the legions those grammarians taught — grind their teeth. When it's easy to fix, we should fix it. It was easy here:

> Mr. Lindsey has said he never asked the bank to not file the disclosure form.

Correctness aside, isn't "not to file" much more natural?

But there are times when we should let the infinitive fanatics grin and bear it. The writer said a business executive "pushed a button to officially activate the assembly lines at the $212 million plant recently." There are alternatives, but "officially" sounds fine where it is, right in the middle of that infinitive.

Agreeing with the thrust of that, Neil Tipton e-mailed to point out an ancillary problem with the example. Said Mr. Tipton, a former newspaper reporter and now a public relations manager for the West Mercia Constabulary (that would be the one in England):

> Surely the writer who was talking about the switching on of assembly lines has still made a glaring (or should that be dangling) error? What, after all, is a "$212 million plant recently?" I think a much better alternative would be for the executive to have "recently pushed a button to officially activate the assembly lines at the $212 million plant."

Agreed. As real estate agents like to remind us, it's all about three words: location, location, location.

# Stadium(s)

See Graffiti/Graffito

# Stanch/Staunch

See Gantlet/Gauntlet

# Straighten/Straiten

### *The Straitened and Narrow?*

The author, his obituary said, had been reticent about his personal life but had told of growing up "in genteel but often straightened circumstances." Unless the point was that the family got the ironing done, the word the writer and editor wanted was "straitened."

That is the participle of "to straiten," meaning to restrict or limit or narrow (think of "strait," a narrow body of water). As an adjective, the participle means limited, restricted, in a tight squeeze.

"Straiten" is a nice word in all its forms and can be applied to life in general, to the atmosphere of an institution, and much else. But the most commonly used form is that participle, and the most common meaning — as it was intended to be for the deceased author — is strapped for cash.

# Such As

See Like/Such As

# Suspect/Suspected (Adjective)

### *Suspecting the Worst*

The article said United Nations inspectors wanted to visit "suspect biological and chemical weapons sites."

Since "suspect" simply means looked on with suspicion, that sentence said that there were in fact biological and chemical weapons sites, and they were in some way suspect.

But the sites' very existence was still unproven, and was the question the inspectors were looking into. The word the writer and editor wanted was "suspected."

# Swatch/Swath

### *Nearly Twins*

"Swath" and "swatch" look alike and sound alike but aren't related, and the wrong one was chosen here:

…they cut a swatch of land and spent nine hours searching…

A swatch is a sample of fabric or leather or a collection of such samples. Think "c" for "cloth" to arrive at the "c" in "swatch."

A swath, which the writer of our example had in mind, is a path cut by something, originally one the width of a scythe stroke.

Figuratively, the way it's more likely to be used nowadays, to cut a swath is to make a big impression or have a well-noted success. But we can think "th" for swath and scythe, anyway.

# Tautology

### *Once Is Enough*

A nice, precise word to remember: tautology. It's a subdivision of redundancy, and it means saying something twice, unnecessarily (and most often unintentionally).

To wit: "The general consensus of opinion seems to be that there is an abundance of choice." Drop "general" and (for goodness' sake) drop "of opinion"; they're already there in "consensus." It's a tidy word meaning a general opinion, and it needs no embellishment.

"Classmate" means a *fellow* member of a class at a school. So when we read that the commencement speaker "drew laughs from his fellow classmates" and a student "used a pellet gun to threaten a fellow classmate" and a character in a play "constantly interrupts the professor and his fellow classmates" and a young lady "encouraged her fellow classmates to keep themselves grounded" and some students don't "have information about fellow classmates," the common thread is — two guesses, and the first one doesn't count.

Other classic tautologies involve the time of day:

> Each morning at 7:45 A.M. ...Most evenings he did not return home until eight o'clock at night.

Whew! "A.M." (for antemeridian or ante meridiem) means before noon; having started with "each morning," we don't have to paint the lily by bringing up "A.M." And having said "Most evenings," we certainly don't want "at night." Yet it's common to read things like "7 P.M. Thursday night" or "9 A.M. yesterday morning." Tautologies all.

Temptations abound. Do we really want to say that "additional restrooms will be added" or that a road project will "add additional lanes"? Or describe someone as a "knowledgeable expert"? Or say an employer requires, or doesn't, "prior experience"? Or (with thanks to Jenn Richardson, copy chief of the *Navy Times,* based in Springfield, Va.) "XX new homes were built"?

Think taut.

*See also Reason Is That.*

# 'That Of,' Omitted

## *Flawed Pairings*

Ken Ashin, a software engineer from Auburndale, Mass., came across That, Omission Of (next up) and thought it might cover "a related subject — the missing 'that of,' as in 'The population of Massachusetts is bigger than Rhode Island.'"

Point taken. The purpose of that sentence isn't to compare a body of people to a geopolitical entity; it's to compare two bodies of people. So we want "The population of Massachusetts is bigger than that of Rhode Island" (or "than Rhode Island's," abandoning parallel construction but sounding less legalese).

The omission of "that of" or an equivalent is a minor error and only rarely leads to confusion, but on occasion the result can be unintentionally funny.

# That, Omission Of

## *What's Wrong with That?*

Jane Greer, an e-mail friend of Language Corner (see Reader's Potpourri) was struck by seemingly odd omissions of the word "that":

> People insist that in college writing classes, adult-ed classes, and professional training classes, instructors are telling them to excise the poor little bugger.

An aversion to "that" does seem conspicuous of late in the public prints, maybe because of a knee-jerk obsession with saving words, maybe just to avoid thinking about whether to use the word. Consider this, about a company named Aristotle:

> ...it is not surprising Aristotle, which was started in 1983...

*What* is not surprising Aristotle? Oops! They didn't mean it that way; they meant it was not surprising *that* Aristotle did such and such.

A novelist committed the same misdemeanor when he had a character say he was "just pointing out the killer probably doesn't care..." It's hard not to misread, momentarily, "just pointing out the killer," and the true meaning emerges only after that hiccup. It's much clearer to say "just pointing out *that* the killer..."

Usually, "that" isn't necessary with "say" in any of its forms. It is generally wanted, though, with many other words of saying

144

— report, announce, believe, insist, suggest, show, declare, point out, and so on — and in constructions like the Aristotle passage cited above. It adds idiomatic roundness and more importantly, as we've seen, it can avoid momentary but irritating confusion.

Delete "that" in Ms. Greer's sentence beginning "People insist," and the reader is misled into thinking that people insist (something) in college writing classes. That's not what Ms. Greer meant and not what the sentence says as she wrote it.

And then this:

> The Gore campaign believed the recount, which is continuing in two counties and pending in one...

But after that lengthy interruption, it turns out the Gore camp believed *that* the recount "could produce enough votes to erase Mr. Bush's small lead." (Note that if the passage said "thought" instead of "believed," no problem would arise whether or not "that" was used.)

> Boras explained his requests...

Actually, he explained *that* "his requests were not contract demands..."

Is there a campaign to get rid of "that," no matter the cost in euphony and clarity? Maybe so, and maybe if we're alert we can stop it. "That" is an awfully small word. We should go ahead and use the space, or the itsy bitsy fraction of a second.

# That/Which

## *Some Things Aren't Essential*

Why "that" in one place and "which" in another? It's an unreasonable burden, but it's there. Here goes:

The cars that were green failed to run.

In that sentence, "that were green" is a restrictive, defining, or (the favorite here) essential clause.

It's essential because without it, we have "The cars failed to run" — not at all what we set out to report. Orange cars, say, may have hummed right along; it was green cars that didn't. Now consider:

The cars, which were green, failed to run.

Take out the clause, and the purpose of the sentence remains intact: the cars — all the cars we're discussing — failed to run. Their color is incidental, not essential.

The principle is the same even if the content of the (nonessential) "which" clause is exciting:

The cars, which exploded in a huge ball of flame, were green.

For *the purpose of the sentence as it's structured*, what is essential is not what happened to the cars but what they looked like: "The cars were green."

Commas are characteristic around "which" clauses but not "that" clauses: He ate three apples, which made him sick, before dinner. In fact, for writers of the British school only the commas make clear what kind of clause we're dealing with.

The Britons' great mentor, H. W. Fowler, favored using "that" in essential clauses and "which" in nonessential, but he has largely been ignored by his countrymen. "Which" occurs routinely in both kinds of clauses in British writing, with no obvious loss of clarity.

This passage, of American origin, was uncomfortable:

...the equivalent of Britain's Official Secrets Act that imposes harsh punishment...

because the writer was not distinguishing this Official Secrets Act from some other. The passage wanted a "which" clause, complete with commas.

Summing up: The that/which rule is arbitrary and overly subtle and ought to be done away with. It is without intrinsic sense, but as long as large numbers of teachers and editors insist on it, we do well to understand it.

## 'The Late'

See Late, as in Dead

## *The* Police

See Police, *the*

## 'They' after Singular Noun

See He or She, etc.; Singular Noun, Plural Pronoun

## 'They Each'

### *Number Notes*

The newspaper reported,

Gov. Christine Todd Whitman and State Senator James E. McGreevey clashed over property taxes and automobile insurance rates tonight during their second televised debate as they each sought to portray themselves as the champions of homeowners and drivers.

Can't have it both ways — "they" and "each" (and then "themselves"). The simplest solution is to delete "each." If both candidates were of the same sex, the singular would work, and it seems a little tidier, somehow: "...as each sought to portray herself..." In any case, "they each sought to portray themselves" doesn't make it.

*See also Collective Nouns, Tons Was.*

# Till/Until

### *A Full Till?*

A colleague had a FAQ, as we say in show biz:

> If "till" is an abbreviated version of "until," why don't we spell it "til" and use an apostrophe – 'til?

"Till" isn't an abbreviation. It's a word in its own right, going back a millennium or so. It's apparently older than "until."

The retention of both words to say precisely the same thing is just one of those loveable idiosyncrasies English glories in.

Some authorities do prefer "until" at the start of a sentence, and that's certainly a safe course. Happily, though, no such notion deterred the folks who brought us the evergreen "Till Then."

# Times as Much/Times More Than

See Oddities

# To Be Sure

See As Such (Transition)

# 'Tons Was'

## *Singular Virtue*

A reader was furious at his local newspaper for having told its readers,

> More than 13 tons of cocaine was found on a fishing boat in the Pacific Ocean.

The letter to the editor was nothing if not stern:

> The fact that you writers and editors do not care about the basics of the language shows that our society has finally reached a level of mediocrity never before accepted.

And more. Whew! But the outrage was misplaced.

The letter-writer thought the sentence should have read "13 tons of cocaine were found..." Plural noun (tons), plural verb — that's the rule, isn't it?

But the article had not reported on the finding of thirteen individual things — thirteen stolen cars, for example. It reported on the finding of a *quantity* of something, cocaine. Rigid adherence to a rule led the indignant reader out the window. The concept the sentence dealt with was singular, and "was found" was preferable by a ton.

The same principle applied here:

> More than $57 million in accumulated taxes and customs duties collected by Israel from Palestinians were supposed to have been transferred.

Despite the plural "taxes" and "duties" that follow, the transferring involved that $57 million. And since we're dealing with the transfer of a sum, not a dollar at a time, it should read "*was* supposed..."

# Too (Starting Sentence)

See As Well As, Too (Starting Sentence)

# Tortuous/Torturous
## *Painful, but Different*

In English a good many words are so similar it's tough to remember how to keep them apart. Often the chore is satisfying and enjoyable — "precipitate" and "precipitous" (which see) come to mind. At the other, irritating extreme are "awhile" and "a while" (which see). Somewhere in between we have "torturous" and "tortuous." Both words come from "torquere," Latin for "to twist" and a grandparent, as well, of "torque."

"Tortuous" means twisting or winding, and used figuratively can refer to complexity, difficulty, or deviousness. The literal meaning certainly seemed to fit "a tortuous gravel road 500 miles long."

"Torturous" — the middle "r" found in "torture" is the mnemonic device for this pair — means torturing or causing harsh pain physically or emotionally, literally or figuratively. It was used well to describe the baseball team "in the middle of a torturous period of 30 games in 30 days."

But sometimes the choice is a coin toss. Something that twists and turns can also be painful (like that gravel road, maybe).

So in a story about a couple of campaigners who had traveled highways and byways with their petitions, a reader might have expected to hear of their "tortuous road" to the ballot.

But they had also "sweltered in the summer heat," among other travails, and the writer was justified in his decision to report that they had "survived a torturous road."

# 'To She and I'

See 'Older than Him'

# To...To

## Small Precision

O nly a visitor from Mars — or maybe Mauritius? — would be confused by this, but in fact it's missing an important word:

> President Bush reached out today to Democrats and moderates in his party...

The missing word is a second "to." It belongs before "moderates." As written, with only the first "to," the sentence can be read to mean there are moderates and Democrats in Mr. Bush's party. Have a look, with an open mind.

Making the passage read "to Democrats and to moderates in his party" would make it clear that Mr. Bush was reaching out to one group outside his party and one group inside it.

In other situations like this one, a reader wouldn't have to be from somewhere far away to be mystified. Nail it down with a double "to."

# Toward(s)

## Two Sides of the Big Pond

J ane Greer (see Reader's Potpourri) e-mailed to say she was puzzled at seeing "towards" in some places and "toward" in others and wanted to know the difference, if any. It's strictly cultural: The British and their followers in style matters use an "s," and Americans don't, at least not in recent decades. Some American writers and editors affect it, and some perpetrate it by mistake, but it looks odd.

# Transition

See 'As Such'

# Troopers/Troupers

## *Support Our Troups?*

From Hannah Feldman, associate editor of *Baltimore Magazine*, a "small question, but it's been plaguing me": Is someone who perseveres in the face of difficulty a real trooper, "akin to calling someone a brave little soldier," or a real trouper, "a professional performer for whom the show must go on, no matter what?"

It's the latter, as Ms. Feldman suspected. Spelled with a "u," and accompanied by an adjective or standing alone, "trouper" denotes a member of a theatrical company (usually traveling, in a troupe) and has come to mean someone who keeps plugging away even when things go sour.

The double "o" spelling is for a soldier — particularly cavalry, as in "F Troop"— or, most commonly in this country, a state police officer. If one of those were to soldier on under tough circumstances, we might say "the trooper was a real trouper." Or we might not.

# Try and/Try to

## *A Trying Idiom*

Phrasings like these pop up a lot:

...to try and curtail the nation's high recidivism rate

...to try and weed out detainees

...to try and discredit Norquist...

It's clear from the e-mail, though, that some percentage of those who read collections like this one are offended by "try and." Their pet-peevishness gets support from some commentators and lexicographers. In conversation or colloquial writing, they say, it's fine, but in serious writing we have to say "try to."

Yet the writing quoted above is serious, and such examples are legion. No distinction between "try and" and "try to" arises from reasonable inference about their meaning (though some supporters of "try and" have argued for a difference).

And there's no question that "try and" is durable. Both "and" and "to" have been used with "try" in all kinds of writing for over 300 years to form both the infinitive, as in our citations, and the imperative (Try and stop me!).

The attack on "try and" arose in the 19th century; defenders of the phrase in the 20th included the immortal H. W. Fowler, hardly a permissive parent.

Perhaps the objection to "try and curtail," for example, stems from a belief that it literally means (1) try and (2) curtail. Such a reading is justifiable (but why bother?) for other verb phrases using "and" — Stop and visit awhile, for example, or Come up and see me sometime, as Mae West didn't exactly say. But with "try and" that reading is an artificial stretch.

It's a peculiar idiom; "and" isn't comfortable with "tries" or any other part of the verb but "try" itself. But it's also a thoroughly established idiom, and we should feel free to use it and stop worrying about it.

# Unique

### *The One and Only*

Bob Howard, a visitor to the *Columbia Journalism Review* Web site and a "cranky old (51 years) journalist who had grammar drilled into him by even crankier schoolteachers and editors," was affronted when he read this in a headline deck:

Inside Southern California's most unique real estate market…

Affronted he should be. As he pointed out, modern dictionaries do accept "highly unusual" or "very rare or uncommon" down on their lists of definitions for "unique." But that's a cave-in.

Look at the start of that word — "un." It means "one" (from the Latin "unus") just as it does in "union" and "united" and "unicorn" and "unit" and…you name it. Something that is unique is one of a kind. It can't be very, or less, or more, or somewhat, or a tad, or most unique. It's unique, period. For weaker intentions, "rare" or "highly unusual" or other words and phrases are readily available.

On this one the cranks — young, old, and in between — have to do battle, as one.

# Use/Usage

## *Use It or Lose It*

"The overall increase in usage," the article said about election-night Internet traffic, "was barely perceptible."

Another report had the local utility saying "electricity demand for the month of June hit a new peak yesterday and nearly set a record for daily usage."

And a sub-headline reported,

Curtailing Energy Usage, City Is a Model of Efficiency

Such employment — which is to say, use — of "usage" threatens one of those nice distinctions we ought to cherish, and there's a lot of evidence in the age of the ether that the cause is desperate.

The word should not be resorted to as a high-hat substitute for "use." The longer word should be saved for situations involving custom or practice or tradition. This glimpse of Mayan civilization exemplified fine usage:

The scribes outdid themselves with at least seven variations of glyphs for the verbal root "to happen," a common usage in monumental inscriptions celebrating victory in battle and other achievements of rulers.

Obviously the authors of our earlier examples didn't mean an increase in some venerable custom on election night, or the practice of electricity, or an energy tradition.

If all we're talking about is using something — consuming, making use of — the noun of choice is "use."

# Utilize

See Reader's Potpourri

# Wangle/Wrangle

## No Wrangle Here

When Mark W. Freeman, a writer, former English teacher in Glens Falls, N.Y., and author of the "Washington County Curmudgeon" column for the *Post-Star* in Glens Falls, read that someone "had been trying to wrangle an invitation," it made him think of Tom Mix's sidekick, the Old Wrangler.

That worthy gentleman worked with livestock; it might be worth remembering, by way of a loose synonym and a mnemonic, that a WRangler might WRestle with unruly critters.

More broadly, "wrangle" means to argue or dispute, with someone or over something:

> While its national bosses wrangle over the PRI's future and their role in it...

> They must wrangle with Mr. Clinton, who usually holds the upper hand in these negotiations.

As a noun the word means an argument, often protracted, as in "a continuing wrangle with the city authorities over money he is owed."

As Mr. Freeman observed, the writer of the original example wanted "wangle," a colloquial word meaning to obtain something by trickery, cajolery, or sheer persistence, the kind of thing people do with invitations. The "r" didn't belong, nor did it in the passage about a man "offended when teams wrangle subsidies for new stadiums and arenas" or in "you'll probably be able to wrangle your best deal at the final show." Make it "wangle" each time.

# Weapon(s) Inspector

## *Stylish Idiom?*

Not long before what came to be called "Operation Iraqi Freedom," an interesting e-mail arrived from K. S. Nayar of *The Gulf Today,* an English-language daily in Sharjah, the United Arab Emirates:

> Which one would you prefer, "weapons inspectors" or "weapon inspectors"?

Two matters of usage come into play in that one. One is idiom, and by then the slightly quirky "weapons" seemed to be thoroughly accepted worldwide.

(Why? Not clear. Why "school board" and "schools chancellor"? The root of "idiom" is a Greek word whose meanings include "peculiar." For what it's worth, the same root gives us "idiot.")

The other usage matter involves style, the choices publications make primarily for consistency's sake. Idiom or no, "weapon inspector" is solidly defensible on grounds of grammar and logic and would be acceptable as a style choice — like "school board," for example. But it would be a lonely position.

# Well, the Adjective

## All's Good that Ends Well?

A few years back, an otherwise bright student in an introductory editing course insisted that there was something wrong with using "well" as an adjective, as in "He isn't well." That was nonsense, but just a personal quirk, it seemed.

Time passed, and the same odd notion turned up in print. "We often tell our friends," the essayist observed with a snicker, " 'You look well,' when not referring to their vision." Only a joke, maybe, but why encourage adolescent literal-mindedness?

"Well" is an adverb, of course: She runs well, he sings well, and maybe for a frontier scout, he looks well.

But the word is also an adjective — a synonym for "healthy" and an antonym for "sick" (and the reason "unwell" exists). Of course we tell our friends, "You look well." And when they're not well, the missives we send them aren't get-good cards.

Though most common nowadays in discussions of health, "well" can also be used as a broader adjective. *Merriam-Webster's Dictionary of English Usage* notes that it has been both adjective and adverb since the time of Alfred the Great. Hardy indeed.

The superstition about "well" seems more widespread than common sense might suggest. Why? A craving for absolutes, perhaps, leading to misguided pedantry. It is well to resist such temptations.

*See also (I Am) Good/(I Am) Well.*

# Whence

## The Whence Offense

It started as a modest little essay. Then came Holy Writ and the Bard.

"Whence," a word usually used in our time for comic or poetic effect, means "from where." That makes "from whence" an irritating tautology:

> But politicians who forget from whence they came...
>
> ...from whence has this buxom cherub descended?
>
> ...from whence came fish and chips?

But then,

> I will lift up mine eyes unto the hills, from whence cometh my help.

That's how the beautiful, much-quoted Psalm 121 begins in the King James and other English-language Bibles and how millions remember it to this day. And *Merriam-Webster's Dictionary of English Usage* notes that the use of "from" with "whence" is ancient and that the users included, in the King James era though less memorably, Shakespeare.

But immortals have special rights (and Shakespeare, the old shark, also gave us "most unkindest cut" in the service of iambic euphony).

About "from whence," the generally wise and wonderful *Merriam-Webster's* concludes,

> We see no great fault in using it where it sounds right, and great writers have used it where it sounds right all along.

Hmph, or something. Let's let "from whence" go. It had its run in the 17th century.

# Where...at

## *The Where Stands Alone*

Bill MacLoughlin of CBC Radio News in Edmonton, Alberta, wondered about what seemed to be a trend:

Maybe I missed something. Suddenly it seems everyone, including anchors, must use the word "at," as in "where is he at?" Where did this little horror come from? Is there any defence?

"Where" with "at" comes from one of two places: ignorance or affectation. It's not only a tautology, it's also a barbarism. Which is to say, it's not English. There we are.

And yes, "defence" is the way to spell it, in Canada and other bastions of British English.

# Wherefore

### *Brush Up Your Shakespeare, Act IV*

Headline about a no-longer-prominent athlete:

O Denis, Denis! Wherefore art thou Denis?

Comment on the fickle pop music world:

Local DJ trends come and go (wherefore art thou, acid jazz?).

Whimsy amid wicked weather:

Wherefore art thou, Romeo? Home with his feet up by the fire, if the poor lad had any luck at all.

All those allusions to Shakespeare are fatally flawed, as "wherefore art" cuteness almost always is. Juliet's plaintive "O Romeo, Romeo! Wherefore art thou Romeo?" has nothing to do with her lover's location.

"Wherefore" means "why" (in both senses — "how come?" and "for that reason"). Juliet is asking why the fates made Romeo part of the Montague family, with which her Capulets were locked in a virulent feud.

"'Tis but thy name that is my enemy," she sighs. If his name had been the Veronese equivalent of Joe Smith, the two of them could have lived happily ever after.

By and large, "wherefore" survives today only in fancy proclamations and petitions, in some legal documents, and in the expression "the whys and wherefores." Also in stagings of *H.M.S. Pinafore* ("Never Mind the Why and Wherefore") and, painfully often, in misaimed Shakespearean allusions.

# Whether (or Not)

## *Murky Whether*

There are writers and editors and teachers out there whose blood boils when they see "or not" after seeing "whether." Terrible waste of words, what?

In fact, "or not" is never wrong; the phrase simply expresses the negative alternative to whatever "whether" is talking about.

Sure, drop "or not" when it's just extra words — constructions like "She wouldn't say whether or not she would run," or "He asked whether or not the ship was sinking." In each case, the alternative represented by "or not" is inescapable and needn't be stated.

At times, though, balance, euphony and even logic demand "or not" or something else to specify the alternative outcome.

On the logic front, the celebrated John B. Bremner noted in his classic *Words on Words* that the little word "if" can be used to test the need for "or not." It means one thing, he noted, to say, "I'll love you whether or not you leave me," and quite another to say, "I'll love you if you leave me." We need "whether or not" to convey the full thought.

More subtly, this sentence needed something to complete — and balance — the thought that "whether" began:

Whether the jawboning and billions of dollars in foreign-exchange intervention succeed in propping up the yen, they will almost certainly succeed in propping up Mr. Hashimoto.

The thought imbedded in "whether" drops off a cliff; the sentence has to say explicitly that the jawboning and so on may *not* save the yen. One way to make the alternative clear would be to add "or fail" after "…intervention succeed." Easier still, we could start with "Whether or not."

But this was a perfect example of a sentence that did not need "or not":

…Mr. Starr must decide whether or not he should seek the indictment of the president.

The phrase contributes nothing to the sense or the sound.

# Whom

## *Doomed? Not Yet*

A lot of smart people hate the word. It can sound stuffy, and, more importantly, it's very easy to get wrong. The great *New York Times* editor and language authority Theodore M. Bernstein, who almost certainly never got it wrong, nonetheless campaigned to "Doom Whom" (except after prepositions). He lost, at the *Times* and in the larger world. For anything approaching formal writing, "whom" clearly will be with us for a good while longer.

The most common who/whom problem arises in sentences where a distraction pops up between the pronoun and the verb it goes with.

For example, an article spoke of a woman bound to "a man whom she knew would never be faithful." The distraction is the little phrase "she knew." It's parenthetical and irrelevant to the choice of a pronoun.

Put parentheses (or commas) on either side of "she knew" — they're not needed, but would not be technically wrong — and it's instantly clear that our pronoun goes with "would never be" and that we wouldn't say "whom would never be faithful."

And think MMMMM: "hiM" and "whoM" (and "whoMever") all work the same way. They are objects. In our example, the verb "would never be" needed a subject, and it had to be "who."

A different challenge:

> …cameras showing whomever was speaking.

The W word might seem to be the object of "showing," but it isn't. The object is the whole three-word clause that follows "showing." Once again, that clause needs a subject to go with its verb. Since we wouldn't say "hiM was speaking," we can't say "whoMever was speaking." It has to be "whoever."

This was a beaut: Game shows, the story said, are

> popular only with older viewers, who advertisers are least interested in reaching.

Which is to say, least interested in reaching they. Make it "whom."

Some other examples; the first two reinforce the importance of ignoring interruptions:

A lot of testimony, the article said, focused on a man "whom the authorities believe masterminded the plot." The trap was "the authorities believe"; put the parentheses around it, or commas, or delete it mentally, and see. It wouldn't be "hiM masterminded the plot," so it can't be "whoM."

In this one, if we do the same exercise with the parenthetical "he believed," the need for "who" becomes obvious:

At Calder, he curbed corruption by summarily exiling from the track dozens of trainers whom he believed were dishonest.

He believed *they* were dishonest, not *them* were dishonest.

And a trickier one, partly because the sentence fails to track, quite apart from the who/whom question:

> The legislative future of the abortion debate is more complicated, related to a pending Supreme Court decision on abortion, on who wins the presidency and who he might nominate to fill Supreme Court vacancies.

"Related to" begins a series that suddenly switches to "on" ("on who wins") as its preposition. Easily fixable. But regardless of the preposition, the first "who" is correct — the *subject* of the clause "who wins the presidency." The second "who" is wrong; the pronoun is the *object* of "nominate." Again, think M: The president might nominate hiM, not he. The sentence should read "whoM he might nominate."

Some might argue for leaving who/whom technically wrong when it sounds natural and the repair would sound like fingernails across a blackboard:

> ...discovering a way to score no matter who Chicago had on the mound.

There (look carefully) the pronoun is the object of "had." We couldn't say "Chicago had he," so only "whom" would satisfy purists. But "no matter whom Chicago had on the mound"? Unkind. If the letter of the law is mandatory in your shop, duck the issue:

> ...no matter who was on the mound for Chicago.

We can break the rule for fun as long as we let the reader in on the gag. To convey astonishment, for example, we might want to say "She married *who*?" It's natural. So is the emphasis provided by the italics; without them, "who" could look like ignorance.

Julie Mulhall e-mailed to tell about producing an ad for WMGM-TV, in Linwood, N.J., that said,

> When you think of news in South Jersey who do you think of?

There was a near-duplicate about the weather. Someone returned both with "whom" substituted for "who."

Ms. Mulhall asked which was correct. Alas — and that's the only word for it — "whom" is correct. We viewers/listeners/readers were expected to think *of* something, and "of," a preposition, takes an object, and an object has to be "whom."

That's hardly a wonderful solution for snappy ad copy (or anything else) but staying with "who" could have given some people the idea it was correct English, and there was no way to signal otherwise. Fortunately, Ms. Mulhall said, it was time for a new slogan anyway.

This passage didn't aspire to the snappy — "He did not mention who else he had in mind" — but it certainly seemed natural. Yet the pronoun had to be the object of "had [in mind]," and that means "whom." Make it "anyone else he had in mind"?

Bernstein was on to something.

# Whose/Of Which

## *'Whose' You Can Use*

A superstition, still rather widely held, may well have been at work here:

> ...in the province, the population of which consists predominantly of ethnic Albanians...

The superstition is that no form of the pronoun "who," which is used for human beings, can stand in for a common noun, like "province," denoting a thing.

That's not so. The use of "whose" for things has been around for centuries (the great H. W. Fowler cited Shakespeare and Milton in its defense) and, in sentences like the one above, is a lot more graceful than the alternative. "Of which" isn't wrong, but it can irritate.

So make it "…in the province, whose population…," save the extra words, and avoid the pain in the ear.

# 'Woof Down'

## *Animal Appetites*

Lisa Aug, a defender of the language from Frankfort, Ky. (see "Lightening"; "Forecasted"), was troubled when an online news site, reporting on an impoverished child's torturous attempt to walk from Nicaragua to the United States, said,

> Mamacitas clean their pans and grills for scraps, which he woofs down.

The expression for avid eating is "wolf down," after the animal of ravenous repute. Outside the weaving and sound-reproduction trades, "woof" is a word for a sound dogs supposedly make and has nothing to do with eating. (The word for such sound-imitating words, good to know and especially handy if a spelling bee comes along, is onomatopoeia.) But a computer search suggests that "woof down" is showing up more than it used to. Sometimes it's junior high school humor in stories about dogs, and we ought to leave such stuff to the junior high school humorists. But sometimes it appears to be sheer error.

Ms. Aug, objecting to "ubiquitous improper usage smothering proper usage," went on,

> To quote my mother, if everybody jumped off a cliff, would you do it too?

Down (as it were) with lemmings!

# You, Understood

## *It Had to Be You*

If someone shouts, "Get out of here!" or murmurs, "Be my guest," we're hearing complete sentences. Their subject, though we can't hear it (or in writing see it), is "you." Why it's valuable to know that is not altogether clear, but occasionally the question comes up.

*See also 'Older than Him'; 'To She and I'*

# Z

There's nothing under Z.